For Samuel and Grace—my life's greatest blessing

Owlkids Books Inc.
10 Lower Spadina Avenue, Suite 400, Toronto, Ontario M5V 2Z2
www.owlkidsbooks.com

Distributed in Canada by University of Toronto Press
5201 Dufferin Street, Toronto, Ontario M3H 5T8

Distributed in the United States by Publishers Group West
1700 Fourth Street, Berkeley, California 94710

Acknowledgments
Thank you to everyone at Owlkids Books, especially John Crossingham for your direction and genuine enthusiasm throughout this project. To Russell Byars, Miles Daisher, and Kris Holm for sharing your expertise. To Brad for your part along the way. And to Mom & Dad, Robert, Rebecca, Abby & Jack, Adele, and Michelle for your unwavering support in all things.

Library and Archives Canada Cataloguing in Publication

Birmingham, Maria
    Weird zone : sports / written by Maria Birmingham.

(Weird zone)
Includes index.
Issued also in electronic format.
ISBN 978-1-926973-60-9 (bound).--ISBN 978-1-926973-61-6 (pbk.)

    1. Sports--Juvenile literature. I. Title. II. Series: Weird zone (Toronto, Ont.)

Library of Congress Control Number: 2012948714

Design: Reactor Art & Design, Barb Kelly, and Stephanie Power

 Canadian Heritage / Patrimoine canadien

 Canadä

 Canada Council for the Arts / Conseil des Arts du Canada

ONTARIO ARTS COUNCIL / CONSEIL DES ARTS DE L'ONTARIO

Ontario
Ontario Media Development Corporation
Société de développement de l'industrie des médias de l'Ontario

We acknowledge the financial support of the Canada Council for the Arts, the Ontario Arts Council, the Government of Canada through the Canada Book Fund (CBF) and the Government of Ontario through the Ontario Media Development Corporation's Book Initiative for our publishing activities.

Manufactured by Printplus Limited
Manufactured in Shenzhen, China, in October 2012
Job #S120900344

A   B   C   D   E   F

 Publisher of Chirp, chickaDEE and OWL
www.owlkidsbooks.com

WeirdZone:
SPORTS

The strangest, funniest, and most daringest events from the world of athletics and beyond!

Written by **Maria Birmingham**

Prepare yourself.

This isn't your **everyday sports book**. Sure, sports like baseball, hockey, basketball, and soccer are awesome.

But enough is enough.

There are lots of **other sports** out there—sports around the world that haven't gotten the recognition or the glory they deserve.

They may be slightly **odd**, a bit **weird**, or, in some cases, just plain **crazy**. But the time has come to prove that these unsung sports are the real deal. **So gear up** as we take to the sky, dive down deep, and scour the planet for some of the **coolest sports** that you've never heard of!

Contents

Chapter 1

Going Solo

When you sign up for these sports, you're *taking a walk* on the **weird** side. From wrestling *with your toes* to carving a path down the side of a **volcano**, get an *all-access pass* to some of the **wackiest** sports for one.

Let's Roll!

IMAGINE YOU'RE STANDING inside a giant plastic ball teetering on the crest of a hill. Suddenly, someone gives it a push. Before you can scream "Don't even think about it," you're hurtling down that grassy slope. Wahoo! You're zorbing! This sport got its start in 1994. That's when two thrill-seekers from New Zealand invented the zorb—an inflatable ball that you climb into. Originally, Andrew Akers and Dwane van der Sluis designed the ball so they could walk on water. The zorb stayed afloat, but the friends found it hard to maneuver. So they decided to head for the hills instead!

zorbing:
the sport of rolling down a hill in a large, inflatable ball

Going Down!

Since its invention, hundreds of thousands of people have gone head over heels for the zorb. In fact, there are zorbing sites all around the world, from Canada to Japan. The zorb itself is made of thick, clear plastic. There are two separate balls that make up this sphere. The outer ball is 2.7 m (9 ft.) in diameter and the inner ball is about 2 m (6.5 ft.) around. In between the balls is a pocket of air that acts like a shock absorber, keeping riders from getting bounced around too much during the head-spinning trip. And to get into a zorb, a rider has to climb through a tunnel-like opening. In you go!

dare to compare

DIAMETER
ZORB: 2.7 m (106 in.)
BASKETBALL: 75 cm (29.5 in.)
SOCCER BALL: 69.5 cm (27.4 in.)
BOWLING BALL: 68.5 cm (27 in.)
TENNIS BALL: 6.8 cm (2.7 in.)
GOLF BALL: 42.7 mm (1.7 in.)
PING-PONG BALL: 40 mm (1.6 in.)

great moments in... zorbing

1999
NASA (National Aeronautics and Space Adminitration) used a zorb ball while researching Mars landings.

2006
The record for the fastest zorb ride is held by Keith Kolver, who reached a speed of 52 kmh (32.3 mph) while zipping down a hill in New Zealand.

SPORT SHORTS

You may think going headlong down a hill would make a zorb rider toss his cookies, but zorbing doesn't make you feel all that queasy. The zorb is so big that the rider inside only makes a complete rotation about every 9 m (30 ft.). And this keeps his lunch from making a return visit...usually.

A typical zorb ride lasts about 40 seconds.

En Garde

finger jousting: a battle to the finish using only your finger

FORGET ABOUT A SWORD. In the sport of finger jousting, the weapon of choice is your index finger. In this finger-friendly activity, opponents lock their right hands together and try to jab each other with their outstretched finger. A jouster can poke an opponent anywhere on the body, except the right arm, and points are awarded for every successful jab. When time's up, the jouster with the most points is the champ. As for putting a finger on when this sport began, that's a tough one. But the ancient Israelites are said to have played a version of jousting called finger spearing.

just for laughs

when finger jousting:

1. Keep fingernails short.

2. Shake opponent's hand before match.

3. No obscene hand gestures if you lose.

when toe wrestling:

1. Keep toenails trimmed.

2. Respect the baby toe. (It'd be a shame to hurt it.)

Put Your Best Foot Forward

You better be prepared to go toe-to-toe with the competition in this sport. Toe wrestling is like arm wrestling...except competitors use their feet. A match begins when two barefooted opponents take positions opposite each other on the "toedium," the mat where all the action happens. Wrestlers lock their big toes together and wait for the referee to cry: "Toes away!" With that, they battle until one of them pins the other's foot to the ground. Supporters of the sport once attempted to have it accepted as an official Olympic sport, but their application was denied. That's "toe-tally" a shame!

👉 INSIDE THE RULE BOOK:

finger jousting

Tally up the points for a finger-jousting match.

Left arm:	1 point
Legs:	1 point
Chest/neck/back:	2 points
Head:	3 points

⚛ the science spot

What's in a name? Get the scoop on what each of your fingers is called.

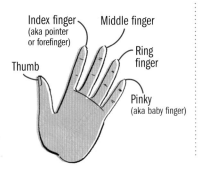

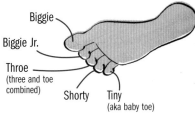

Note: Our toes don't have proper names. So let's throw these out and see if they catch on.

Take a Swing

pillow fighting: a spectator sport where you let your pillow do the talking

EVERYBODY LOVES A GOOD PILLOW FIGHT—that perfect "whack," the laugh-til-it-hurts chaos, the sweet taste of victory. But today's battles aren't just fought at slumber parties. Pillow-fighting has slugged its way into the sports world with events like the Pillow Fight World Cup. In this competition, two contestants let their pillows do the talking. A fighter gets one point every time she hits her opponent's body or head. And she loses a point if her hand or pillow touches the floor. When a competitor ends up on the ground, she's "knocked out." Gotcha!

At a Glance

Use this list to prepare a pillow fight for the ages.

- ☑ Room with no breakables nearby.
- ☑ Ample supply of pillows for all friends.
- ☑ Only soft, fluffy pillows that won't hurt anything...except your pal's pride.
- ☑ A group of fun-loving friends ready for a workout.

I'll have one pillow fighter to go please!

In 2009, a hotel in London, England, offered pillow fights to their guests. With one call to room service, two hotel employees showed up to your room wearing PJs and carrying pillows. The guest could choose one employee to fight and one to referee. Ready, aim, swing...

HERE'S TO HISTORY

Rest your head on these facts about pillows through the years.

- Pillows have been traced back to the ancient Egyptians. Since the Egyptians believed the head was a sacred part of the body, they put elaborate detailing on pillows for the dead.

- The ancient Chinese believed that soft pillows robbed the body of energy, so their pillows were hard boxes made of stone, wood, metal, and ceramic.

- Until the mid-1800s, many people believed it was best to sleep propped up by several pillows in an upright position, and not lying down.

are you serious?

Israeli artist Nelly Agassi created a piece of art that's just a room filled by a gigantic bed. Agassi's masterpiece, *Bedroom*, is a huge wooden bed frame covered with pillows, mattresses, and quilts. Perfect spot for your next pillow fight!

Surf's UP!

IT'S CALLED VOLCANO SURFING, ash boarding, or volcano boarding. But, whatever you call it, it's extreme. Brave riders make a 45-minute trek up a steep—and active!—volcano. Then, once at the top, they hurtle down the mountain on a thin plywood board. The sport, which got its start in 2005, was the brainchild of an Australian man named Darryn Webb. His company set up shop on the slopes of Nicaragua's Cerro Negro. This Central American mountain is covered in volcanic ash from an eruption in 1999—the perfect conditions for the ultimate surfing experience.

volcano surfing:
1. find volcano
2. surf down it

Sit on It... or Not

How fast a volcano surfer flies down the mountainside depends mainly on his technique. Those with a need for speed conquer the volcano while sitting on the sled-like board. They'll whip down the charcoal-black ash at speeds of over 80 kmh (50 mph). If surfers want to experience a slower ride, they can try standing on the board. This way, speeds are closer to 10 kmh (6 mph).

the science spot

Get Moving!

Can you outrun lava flowing from a volcano? The short answer is: Yes. While movies conjure up images of lava spewing from a volcano and burning everything in its path, this hot stuff flows quite slowly. It's much thicker than other liquids and travels at just a few kilometers, or miles, an hour. So, chances are, you can walk faster than lava flows.

Can't Stand the Heat? Too Bad, It's a Volcano!

A volcano is an opening, or vent, in the Earth's surface that allows molten rock, volcanic ash, and gases to escape from the interior. Deep below the surface, the temperature is so hot that rock melts and becomes a liquid rock called magma. This magma rises to the surface and eventually some of it erupts through the vent. Now called lava, it can reach temperatures of 1,200°C (2,200°F). Hot stuff!

HERE'S TO HISTORY

Red-hot details on famous eruptions.

VESUVIUS: This volcano is best known for its eruption in 79 AD, which buried the Roman cities of Pompeii and Herculaneum.

KRAKATAU: This Indonesian volcano's eruption in 1883 was so loud it could be heard 4,800 km (3,000 mi.) away.

MOUNT PELÉE: An active volcano located in the Caribbean, Mount Pelée erupted in 1902. Minutes later, a town of 30,000 was completely destroyed.

MOUNT ST. HELENS: Residents near this volcano in Washington State were stunned by this volcano's eruption in May of 1980. That's because it hadn't erupted in 123 years.

SPORT SHORTS

The main danger with volcano surfing is falling and getting cut on the rough surface of the mountain. For this reason, surfers must wear protective gear. The hot trends in volcano-surfing apparel include orange jumpsuits, goggles, knee pads, sturdy boots, and helmets.

Boing! Boing! Boing!

extreme pogo: it's the bounce that counts

THERE'S NOTHING LIKE DEFYING GRAVITY. Enter the pogo stick. This super-springy toy has been around for decades. But the fun and games with pogos really took off around the year 2000. That's when new and improved pogo sticks were designed. These pogos allowed riders to soar to heights of over 2.4 m (8 ft.) and made it possible to execute tricks, flips, and acrobatics. This catapulted extreme pogo—or xpogo, for short—into the world. Since 2004, athletes attend the Pogopalooza World Championships to compete in events such as biggest air, most jumps per minute, and best trick.

Take this quiz
Can you match these pogo tricks to their wacky names?

A. The Candy Bar
B. The Coffin
C. The Flamingo
D. The Tick-Tock

Answers: 1. B. 2. D. 3. A. 4. C

invention dimension

This pogo takes its rider to new heights...
make that depths. It's designed to be used
under water. Instead of a spring, this bouncer
has a water-filled ball at its base, which lets
you hop off the walls and floor of a pool.
Glub...bounce...glub!

RECORD BREAKER!

An American man named Ashrita Furman
once set a world record by jumping on a pogo
stick for a distance of 37.18 km (23.11 mi.) in
12 hours and 27 minutes. Guess he really likes
the pogo stick because he later set a record for
crossing the bottom of a pool on one, too!

are you serious?

Two Australian men created
a piece of artwork using
nothing but pogo sticks and
some paint. The pair laid out
a canvas, dipped the end of
their pogo sticks into paint,
and then got hopping!

19

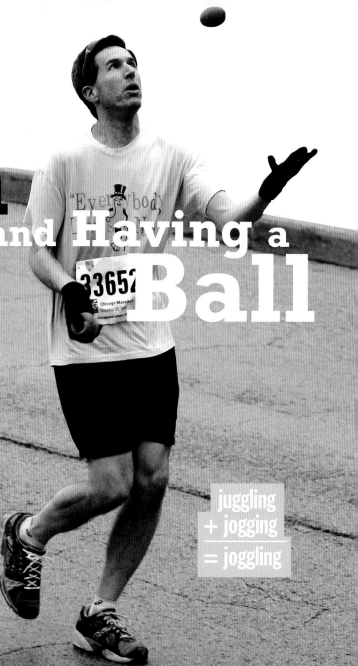

On the
Run
and Having a
Ball

IT'S ONE PART JOGGING and one part juggling. Welcome to the competitive sport of joggling. While it sounds like a pastime only a clown would enjoy, there are athletes—aka jogglers—who take this sport very seriously. In fact, World Joggling Championships have been held each year since 1980. Jogglers put their best foot forward in races that range from 100 meters to 5 kilometers long. And the rules are simple. Juggling must be kept up while jogging. If a ball is dropped, the joggler must return to the place where it fell and continue from there. Keep it up!

juggling
+ jogging
= joggling

How to... Juggle

Before you can joggle, you've got to juggle!

1. Use three soft balls. Hold one ball in right hand. Throw it up so it reaches about eye level and catch it with left hand. Throw it up again, this time catching it with right hand. Practice this.

2. Now hold a second ball in left hand. Toss ball in your right hand, and when it reaches eye level, toss up ball in left hand.

3. Catch first ball with left hand and second with your right.

4. When ready, try juggling a third ball by holding two balls in your right hand. Toss one ball from your right hand. When it reaches eye level, throw the ball in your left hand and catch first ball as you did in step 3.

5. While second ball is in the air, throw third and continue. You should always have at least one ball in the air, and never have more than one ball in either hand.

At a Glance

Top Tips for Joggling (without wobbling!)

☑ *Check your route for obstacles that may slip you up and tie your shoelaces tight. Nothing ends a joggle faster than a nosedive.*

☑ *Don't focus on the balls. Try to look through them. You need to keep an eye on your surroundings.*

☑ *Don't try to do anything else while joggling, like chewing gum or listening to music. You're already doing two things at once!*

☑ *If you drop a ball, quickly grab it and move to the side before rejoining the race. You don't want to be a hazard to those behind you.*

Want to show off your juggling skills? World Juggling Day is held in the middle of June every year. It's a day for jugglers to get together and celebrate their attention-grabbing talent.

the science spot

It turns out even robots like to clown around. In June 2011, scientists at a university in Prague unveiled a robot that can juggle. In fact, the brilliant 'bot can juggle up to five balls at a time.

Sailing through the Skies

SURE, YOU CAN KAYAK on a quiet lake. But wouldn't it be more fun to jump out of a plane while sitting in one, and coming in for a water landing? OK, maybe "fun" is the wrong word. "Terrifying beyond belief" is probably more like it. Skyaking is an extreme sport that combines skydiving and kayaking. It's so extreme that only one person has ever done it. American Miles Daisher invented the sport in July 2002, and he's been freefalling through the sky at speeds of 160 kmh (100 mph) ever since.

skyaking:
the sport of skydiving
with a kayak

Here's the scoop on skyaking from planet Earth's only skyaker, Miles Daisher.

Q: How did you come up with skyaking?
A: Scott Lindgren, who makes kayaking movies, asked me if I could jump a kayak out of an airplane. I tried it, and it worked.

Q: How many times have you gone skyaking so far?
A: I have done 52 skyak jumps thus far. A full deck of cards!

Q: How do you go about jumping out of an airplane in a kayak?
A: First you have to pick the right kayak to jump—a smaller riverboat with a nice bottom. Then you modify your skydiving gear, so your parachute will open while you fly a boat with an extra-large surface area. You put on your parachute. After riding an airplane up at least 1,500 m (5,000 ft.)—4,000 m (13,000 ft.) is preferred—you get in the skyak and close your skirt (the waterproof barrier that wraps around the cockpit of a kayak). When the door of the jump plane opens and you are ready, you scooch out and start to fly.

Q: Can you explain how it feels to skyak?
A: When skydiving, your body on the air is somewhat like swimming on a bed of oxygen. Skyaking is very similar only it's pretty tricky to balance and stay upright. Once you find the boat's sweet spot, it will ride easily. You have to fly your arms for balance and use your hips to maneuver the boat into position.

Q: Are you ever scared while skyaking?
A: It's a bit scary every time I jump, as different things can happen when the wind hits the boat.

Take to the Sky

Forget surfing the waves. Try surfing the air. In skysurfing, a skydiver straps her feet to a skyboard (which is similar to a snowboard) and performs tricks as she falls. And just to make sure the diver doesn't get too lonely while she plummets, she brings a teammate along, known as a camera flyer. As the skysurfer spins, twists, and surfs, the camera flyer records the stunts with a camera that's mounted to his helmet.

MR ADVEN

sky surfing: when surfing on waves just doesn't cut it anymore

SPORT SHORTS

- A skysurfer always wears two parachutes just in case one fails. Phew!
- A skyboard weighs less than 2.3 kg (5 lb.).
- A skysurfing team spends about 50 seconds in the air.

Take this quiz
Can you match each stunt with its description?

1. INVISIBLE MAN

2. THE HELICOPTER

3. THE TIDY BOWL IN THE HOLE

4. THE HAIRY ARMPIT

5. THE TORPEDO

A. The skysurfer holds the camera flyer's feet. Then the camera flyer swings around and stands on top of the board.

B. The surfer falls headfirst while grasping the end of the board.

C. The skysurfer falls in a head-down position and spins.

D. The surfer tucks his arms in and begins spinning so quickly that it's hard to see him clearly.

E. As the skysurfer spins while upside down, the camera flyer flies over and films from above.

Answers: 1. D; 2. C; 3. E; 4. A; 5. B

23

Ready for Take-Off

THE TIME HAS COME to make like Superman. Wingsuit flying is a relatively new activity where skydivers jump from an airplane and glide through the air...all while dressed in a wacky looking get-up called a wingsuit. The wingsuit, which first appeared on the skyward scene in the late 1990s, has fabric between the legs and under the arms to catch air and help its wearer sail along at altitudes of 9,000 m (30,000 ft.). While the suit is perfectly built for flying, it makes for an extremely bumpy landing. That's why wingsuit fliers wear a parachute that they eventually deploy. Better safe than "splat"!

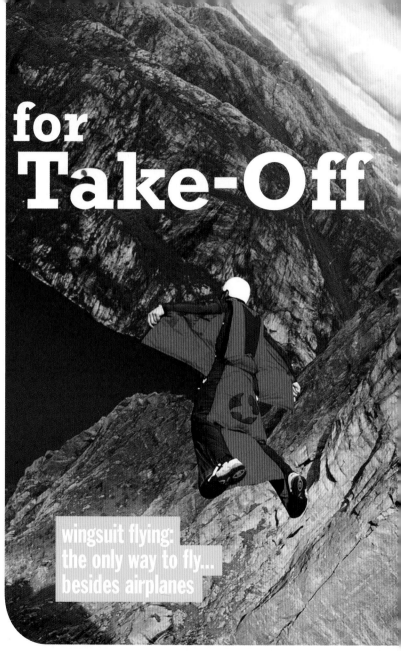

wingsuit flying: the only way to fly... besides airplanes

How to...
Fly in a Wingsuit

1. After jumping from airplane, spread arms and legs to fully open the suit's wings.
2. To turn, twist legs, hips, shoulders, or feet.
3. Only make small movements. A sudden, radical maneuver may force you into a dive or spin. Uh-oh.

BONUS TIP: Don't forget to pull your chute when the time is right!

dare to compare

There's something familiar about a wingsuit. Perhaps it's that it looks an awful lot like the body of a flying squirrel. Let's do a quick comparison:

Wingsuit:
webbed wings between the legs and under the arms allow flier to glide through the air

VS

Flying squirrel:
furry membranes between wrists and ankles help the squirrel "fly" from tree to tree

SPORT SHORTS

- A regular skydiver generally flies at 193 kmh (120 mph). But a wingsuit slows a flier down to an average speed of 80 to 95 kmh (50 to 60 mph).

- A Swiss man named Ueli Gegenschatz once jumped from an airplane in his wingsuit and soared through the big blue sky for an amazing 18 km (11 mi.).

HERE'S TO HISTORY

EARLY 11TH CENTURY	1930s	MID 1990s	1998	2008
An Englishman named Eilmer of Malmesbury attaches wings to his hands and feet and jumps from a tower. Unfortunately, the wind causes him to fall and he breaks his legs. Ouch.	Several men try different wing designs and use a variety of materials, including wood, canvas, and steel, to create wingsuits. Many of these "birdmen" fail to fly, but they inspire future fliers.	French skydiver Patrick de Gayardon creates a wingsuit by placing wings between his legs and arms. This design becomes the basis for modern wingsuit designs.	Jari Kuosma of Finland and Robert Pečnik of Croatia design a wingsuit based on the one invented by de Gayardon and sell their suits to the public.	A Swiss pilot named Yves Rossy becomes the first person to fly a rocket-powered wingsuit. He jets his way across the English Channel at 299 kmh (186 mph).

Two for the Price of One

chessboxing: a sport in which you play a game of chess and throw in a few rounds of boxing for good measure

USUALLY WHEN A BOARD GAME ENDS in fisticuffs, it's a sign that someone's a major sore loser. But, believe it or not, there are times when board games and coming to blows is all part of the fun. Chessboxing is a sport that combines boxing with chess. A match starts with a round of chess, followed by a three-minute round of boxing, and so on. A winner is decided by either checkmate in a chess round or a knockout in the boxing round, whichever happens first.

At a Glance

Take a look at this lowdown of both chess and boxing:

	When was it invented	Object of the game	Equipment needed
CHESS	1475	to checkmate your opponent's king, meaning there is no way to move or defend the piece	square, checkered board, as well as 16 chess pieces
BOXING	688 BC	to knock out your opponent	boxing ring, hand or wrist wraps, and boxing gloves

Take this quiz

Match each boxing move with its proper name.

1. BOB & WEAVE   3. BLOCKING   5. HOOK

2. UPPERCUT   4. JAB

A. a quick, straight punch thrown with one hand

B. a punch that's thrown in a semicircle and is usually aimed at the chin. Also known as a knockout punch.

C. a punch that's directed upward with a bent arm and is aimed at an opponent's chin

D. when a boxer moves from side to side and backward and forward to avoid being hit

E. when a boxer uses his or her shoulders, hands, or arms to protect against incoming punches

Answers: 1. D; 2. C; 3. E; 4. A; 5. B

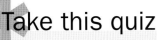

HERE'S TO HISTORY

So whose bright idea was it to combine chess and boxing? Funnily enough, a French cartoonist named Enki Bilal created a comic book in 1992 that introduced the sport. That inspired Dutch artist Iepe Rubingh to bring chessboxing into the real world. In 2003, he organized the first world championships, and the sport has continued to grow in popularity since then.

great moments in...
chess and boxing

CHESS: February 10, 1996

IBM chess computer named Deep Blue defeats reigning world champion Garry Kasparov in a game of chess. Marks first time a computer defeats a world champ at a tournament.

BOXING: January 6, 1681

First recorded boxing match takes place in England. A man named Christopher Monck arranges a bout between his butler and butcher. The butcher is victorious. (Tough luck, Jeeves.)

27

There's a **Reason** They Say It's Tough

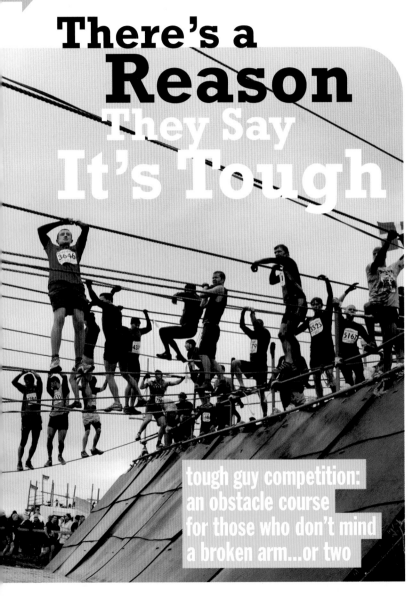

tough guy competition: an obstacle course for those who don't mind a broken arm...or two

BRING ALONG THE BANDAGES! The Tough Guy Competition is said to be the harshest race in the world. It's held every January on a 600-acre farm in England, and it attracts 6,000 guys and gals from around the planet. The day begins with a cross-country run that's followed by a brutal obstacle course. The course is so difficult that about one-third of all competitors can't finish it. Another sign that the day is no walk in the park? Before beginning, participants sign a "death warrant" accepting the risks of the contest. Can you say: "I'll pass"?

Take a Walk on the Wild Side

The lowdown on a few Tough Guy events:

- BEFORE THE OBSTACLE COURSE, competitors complete a 10 km (6 mi.) cross-country run. Then, they try these obstacles:

- THE TIGER: 12 m (40 ft.) high structure made of phone poles, electrified wires, and rope

- FIERY HOLES: Series of muddy ditches with burning bales of hay along the way

- DEAD LEG SWAMP: Swamp of knee-deep mud

- SKY WALK: High nets draped across ice-cold pond

- UNDERWATER TUNNEL: Tunnel of logs in muddy, cold water. (Air holes are provided along the way, for those who need to catch their breath.)

- DEATH PLUNGE: 30 m (98 ft.) high platform that leads to a plank, before a plunge back into bone-chilling water

- DRAGON POOLS: Series of ropes that stretch across a frigid pond. Racers must balance on the ropes as they cross.

So what's in it for the winner of the Tough Guy Competition? No prize money. Just bragging rights!

Take this quiz
Would You Rather?

So what kind of obstacles would you be willing to face?

1. Race through ice-cold water or across hot coals?
2. Swim in a pool full of worms or spiders?
3. Climb a rope coated with mold or slime?
4. Jump through a ring of fire or balance on a beam four stories in the air?
5. Crawl through a pitch-black tunnel or a stinky swamp?
6. Ride a bike through knee-deep mud or off a plank suspended over water?
7. Climb up a hill of smelly socks or smelly cheese?

Flat Out Fun

HOUSEHOLD CHORES and sports don't usually go hand in hand. (If they did, it'd make earning an allowance so much cooler.) That's what makes extreme ironing so outrageous. For this overly unusual sport, people carry an ironing board to a remote location and iron an article of clothing. Of course, since the iron isn't plugged in, there's no real ironing going on. But according to the official rules, you're considered an "ironist"—that's what you call a participant in this sport—if you take a photo or recording of yourself using an iron and ironing board outdoors.

extreme ironing: this is what happens when household chores leave the house

great moments in...
extreme ironing

This im-*press*-ive sport got its start in England in 1997 when a man named Phil Shaw decided to take his ironing with him when he went rock climbing. (We're guessing he was a little bored!) Today, the sport has participants all over the world, and there's even an annual Extreme Ironing World Championship.

2001 A group of 173 scuba divers from the Netherlands set a record for the most people extreme ironing under water.

2003 Australian Robert Fry brings his ironing paraphernalia up into the Blue Mountains near Sydney, Australia. Then, with a parachute strapped to his back, he jumps off a cliff and irons on the way down!

2007 Polar explorer Henry Cookson drags an iron and ironing board to the most remote spot on the planet—the exact center of Antarctica. Brrr...

2011 Two British men named Ben Gibbons and John Roberts reach Base Camp One on Mount Everest with an ironing board in tow. It takes 17 days of climbing, and the men iron a British flag once they arrive.

are you serious?

Extreme ironing has inspired another off-the-wall activity—extreme cello playing. You know the cello—that large musical instrument that looks like a big violin and has to be propped up on the ground. Well, a group of three musicians who call themselves the Extreme Cellists decided to put a musical spin on extreme ironing. They take their cellos to strange locations, like rooftops and mountaintops, and knock out some tunes. That's one way to hit a high note!

just for laughs

Here's a thought. If ironing can be turned into a sport, then why can't we do the same for vacuuming?

31

Go Fly a Kite

kite fighting: it's child's play with a twist

SWOOSH! A KITE GLIDES THROUGH THE SKY, drifting up and down with the wind. Suddenly, another kite swoops in and slices its line. Away it goes! It's just another day at the park in the world of kite fighting, where the object is to cut your opponent's kite line and set it loose. This sport is particularly popular in Afghanistan, Pakistan, India, Nepal, and Korea. Some contests involve hundreds of kite flyers, and the winner is the last one flying. So just how do fighters down a fellow competitor's kite? Many coat their lines with glue and finely crushed glass. Others attach metal shards to their lines. And still others use a strong metallic line or razor-sharp wire instead.

SPORT SHORTS

- Many people chase down the kites that are cut loose. In fact, there's even a name for this pastime: kite running. People of all ages try to track down the runaway kites, some using poles or broken tree branches. Follow that kite!

- Some forms of kite flying don't involve cutting an opponent's line at all. In capture competitions, participants try to snag the other person's kite and bring it down to the ground. And, in a North American version of the sport called line touch, two players go head-to-head with their kites. A judge yells out "top" or "bottom," and the fighters must touch that part of their opponents' line with their airborne kite. Points are awarded to a successful flyer.

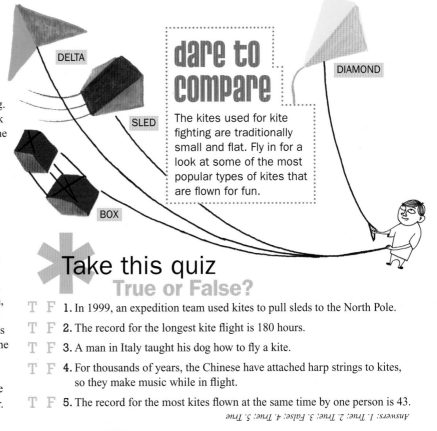

DELTA

DIAMOND

SLED

BOX

dare to compare

The kites used for kite fighting are traditionally small and flat. Fly in for a look at some of the most popular types of kites that are flown for fun.

Take this quiz
True or False?

T F **1.** In 1999, an expedition team used kites to pull sleds to the North Pole.

T F **2.** The record for the longest kite flight is 180 hours.

T F **3.** A man in Italy taught his dog how to fly a kite.

T F **4.** For thousands of years, the Chinese have attached harp strings to kites, so they make music while in flight.

T F **5.** The record for the most kites flown at the same time by one person is 43.

Answers: 1. True; 2. True; 3. False; 4. True; 5. True

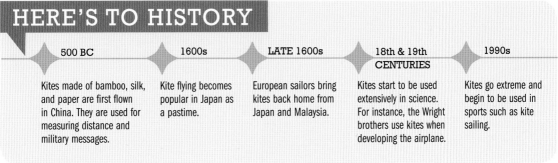

HERE'S TO HISTORY

500 BC	1600s	LATE 1600s	18th & 19th CENTURIES	1990s
Kites made of bamboo, silk, and paper are first flown in China. They are used for measuring distance and military messages.	Kite flying becomes popular in Japan as a pastime.	European sailors bring kites back home from Japan and Malaysia.	Kites start to be used extensively in science. For instance, the Wright brothers use kites when developing the airplane.	Kites go extreme and begin to be used in sports such as kite sailing.

You'll Never See This at the Olympics

Track and field events are considered some of the oldest sporting competitions around. In fact, throwing events like javelin and discus were part of the ancient Olympic Games. But today people are tossing aside the javelin and discus, replacing them with UFOs—unusual flying objects!

BLACK PUDDING THROWING

First things first. Black pudding is a type of sausage. Now that you know that culinary tidbit, let's get to the facts on the World Black Pudding Throwing Championships. This contest is held in Stubbins, England. Contestants toss pieces of black pudding—underhand only—at a stack of muffins. Whoever knocks over the most muffins nabs a cash prize.

BOOT THROWING

The town of Taihape in New Zealand holds an annual Gumboot Day Festival. (FYI—Gumboots are heavy rubber boots.) The main event at the celebration is—what else?—a boot-throwing competition. The person who lobs the footwear the farthest wins the Golden Gumboot trophy.

COW CHIP THROWING

Mooove over! It's the World Cow Chip Throwing Championship. What exactly is a cow chip, you ask? It's a dried piece of cow poop, of course. Every April since 1970, contestants from all over the world have gathered in Beaver, Oklahoma, to see who can pitch the poop the farthest.

34

CUSTARD PIE THROWING

In the World Custard Pie Championships, participants split up into teams and try to hit their opponents with cream pies. In this baked battle, judges award points for hits: six points for a hit squarely on the face, three points for the shoulders or head, and one point for any other body part. Gotcha!

CELL PHONE THROWING

The Cell Phone Throwing World Championships soared onto the scene in Finland in the year 2000. Competitors throw the provided phones with an over-the-shoulder toss or they can fling it freestyle. The winner is the competitor with the longest distance phone call... er, I mean, toss!

EGG THROWING

The World Egg Throwing Championships are held annually in Lincolnshire, England. In one competition, a person throws an egg to a partner, who has to catch it without breaking it. In a second challenge, contestants build catapults and launch eggs to a teammate. If the partner misses the flying fare, the yolk's on him!

MOON ROCK THROWING

The World Moon Rock Throwing Championships are held every two years in Richmond, Australia. Contestants throw round hunks of limestone, known as moon rocks, as far as possible. The rocks, which are common in the area, weigh in at about 30 kg (66 lb.)!

RUBBER CHICKEN THROWING

At the Iowa State Fair, contestants take part in a rubber chicken throwing contest. The object is to toss the flimsy birds as far as possible. Participants stand behind the "fowl line" before they launch the chickens. Then they let the rubber birds fly.

Chapter 2

Go Team!

These team sports are unlike any you ever played in gym class. For example, how many times have you taken part in a *hockey game while seated on a unicycle*? Or built a *tower of people* that's 10 stories high? We'll go out on a limb and say **"never!"** Join the squad and check out these **bizarre** team sports.

On a Roll

unicycle hockey:
one wheel,
one ball,
game on

COMMON SENSE TELLS YOU that bikes and hockey probably aren't a good mix, right? Enter unicycle hockey. This sport first rolled into sight in 1925 when a German silent movie featured two unicyclists playing hockey. But it wasn't until the 1960s that people actually started playing organized games. A unicycle hockey team consists of five players and no goalie. Players use regular hockey sticks and a tennis ball instead of a puck. Plus, there's no contact in this version of hockey. He shoots, he rolls!

great moments in...
unicycling

2002
An American man named Lars Clausen rolled away with the record for the longest unicycle journey. He traveled 14,686.82 km (9,125.97 mi.) by unicycle between April and November. Pedal power!

....

2004
A man named Sem Abrahams rides a wicked tall unicycle. The one-wheeler measured an unreal 35 m (115 ft.) tall. Abrahams had to be lifted to the bike by a crane, and safety cables were attached to the one-of-a-kind unicycle...just in case!

....

invention dimension

It turns out you don't have to unicycle alone. British cyclists Gavin Turk and Ben Wilson have created a four-person unicycle. The 4H uses traditional unicycles that are joined together by a frame.

☞ INSIDE THE RULE BOOK:

Unicycle hockey

- In a unicycle hockey match, there are two 15-minute periods.
- Sticks cannot be used to trip players.

How to...Ride a Unicycle

Need a little help staying put on a unicycle? Mountain unicyclist Kris Holm offers his tips on how to keep upright while you roll. Believe it or not, Holm rides his unicycle everywhere a mountain bike can go, including rugged paths and trails. (Don't forget your helmet!)

1. Find a safe, flat surface with a fence or wall for support. Avoid grass, gravel, and uneven surfaces.

2. Rotate wheel so pedal in the rear is slightly lower than horizontal. Put the saddle between your legs.

3. Grasp the fence or wall with both hands, put your foot on the rear pedal, and rock up onto the unicycle. Sit up straight with most of your weight on the seat. Don't panic—it'll feel unstable at first.

4. Rock back and forth and see how your balance changes. Lean slightly forward, and start pedaling. Look ahead, not at your feet.

5. When you feel comfortable, try letting go of the wall or fence for short distances.

6. Above all, stick with it!

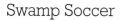

Good, Clean
(make that dirty)
Fun

swamp soccer: it's the beautiful game, only covered in mud

IT'S TIME FOR THE DIRT on swamp soccer. As you might have guessed, this oddball sport doesn't bother with a field. It's played in bogs and swamps. Originally, the game was used as a form of exercise by soldiers. But in 1997, a Finnish man named Jyrki Väänänen started the Swamp Soccer World Championships. Since then, players from near and far have been hitting the sludge for this mud-spattered version of soccer. In fact, there are over 200 teams around the world.

A Mess of Mud

While the rules for swamp soccer are similar to the traditional game, there are some differences on account of all that mud. For example, throw-ins, corner kicks, and free kicks have to be taken by dropping the ball onto your foot. And when it comes to skills, those who know how to use their head often come out on top in swamp soccer. That's because a soccer ball doesn't roll very far in the deep mud, so a header is often the best way to move the ball forward.

A swamp is a piece of land where water doesn't drain well, which leaves the ground wet and mushy.

SPORTS TO SPARE

Playing in sludge is all the rage at the Mud Olympics in Germany. Played along the banks of a river near Hamburg, this dirt-defying event has been held each year since 1978. The day features activities like relay races, soccer, and handball—all played in knee-deep mud.

At a Glance

The real difference without and with mud!

	Year it was first played	Number of players on field	Conditions of field	Playing time	Uniforms	Post-game cleanup
SOCCER	2nd and 3rd centuries BC	maximum of 11, including goalie	well-kept natural grass is ideal	two 45-minute halves	players wear a team shirt, shorts, socks, cleats, and shin guards	a quick shower should do the trick
SWAMP SOCCER	first tournament held in 1997	maximum of 6, including goalie	squishy, deep mud is crucial	two 12-minute halves	players on each team must wear the same color shirts	jump in a nearby river–good luck getting clean!

41

A Maddening Crowd

WHAT DO YOU GET WHEN YOU THROW a ball into a crowd of hundreds of players? Utter chaos...and a crazy sport known as Royal Shrovetide Football. Since at least the 12th century, this two-day game has been played every spring in Derbyshire, England. Each day at 2 p.m., a cork-filled ball is tossed to the masses waiting in the middle of town. Two teams fight to get the ball to their team's goal, which is actually a stone in the middle of the river. (Seriously.) Of course, that's easier said than done since the goals are 5 km (3 mi.) apart! (Again, seriously!)

royal shrovetide football: with hundreds of players on each side, this event takes "team sport" to a whole new level

Rock On!

To move the ball through town, teammates gather together in a large group, called a hug, and try to push against the opposition. The ball is rarely ever kicked, although players can kick, carry, or throw it. When a player reaches his goal, he must hit it against the rock three times in a row. Play ends for the day when a goal is scored...unless that happens before 5 p.m., and then a new ball is released back in the town center, so the match can continue a while longer. (Yes, this is really truly the way the game is played!)

Spectators of this wild scramble of a game are a dedicated bunch.

At a Glance

Shopkeepers board up their stores before the two-day match begins...just in case!

Cars are parked well out of sight, so they aren't damaged during the mayhem of the game days.

👉 INSIDE THE RULE BOOK:

- Ball may not be carried inside a motor vehicle.
- Ball may not be hidden in a bag, coat, or backpack.
- No unnecessary violence is allowed.
- Cemeteries and churchyards are strictly out of bounds.
- Playing after 10 p.m. is forbidden.

talk the talk

If you happen to find yourself caught up in the chaos of Royal Shrovetide Football, here are some terms that'll keep you in the loop.

TURNER-UP: the person who throws out the ball at the beginning of the game

HUG: the large group of players that gather together as they battle for the ball

BREAK: when the ball is released from the hug and play moves quickly

GOALED: instead of saying that a goal is scored, players say the ball is "goaled"

RUNNER: the player that waits outside the hug for the ball. If he gets the ball, he races off for his team's goal.

RIVER PLAY: term used when play ends up in the river. It's possible for the entire game to be played solely in the river.

SHROVIE: short-form for the word Shrovetide

Leaps and Bounds
Above
the Rest

A SPORT THAT'S PLAYED on a bouncy castle? All right, maybe calling it a bouncy castle is a bit of a stretch. But the newfangled sport called bossaball is played on a huge inflatable court. Bossaball is a combination of soccer, volleyball, and gymnastics. Created by Belgian Filip Eyckmans in 2004, it bounced onto Spanish beaches in the summer of 2005. And it's currently a big hit on the beaches of Spain and Brazil.

bossaball:
a volleyball-like sport that's played on an inflatable court

Put Some Bounce into It

Bossaball is played by two teams of three, four, or five players. And the inflatable court is divided in half by a net. One player on each team, called the attacker, stands on an extra-springy trampoline that's built into the court near the net. The rest of the players are positioned around the attacker. To score points, players must ground the ball on the other team's side of the court, sort of like volleyball. What makes bossaball different from volleyball is that the players can use any part of their bodies to get the ball over the net.

are you serious?

Referees are optional in bossaball, but they sure add to the fun. That's because bossaball referees don't just show up with a whistle and make important calls—they bring along a microphone and a DJ set, too. That's right, these "samba referees" spin vinyl!

the equipment

1. Inflatable Court: if a ball drops on the court, the opposing team gets one point.
2. Net: the ball goes over it, not under!
3. Trampoline: each side of the court has a built-in trampoline. The attacker stands on the trampoline, which allows him or her to bounce super high and spike the ball over the net. If a ball drops here, the opposing team gets three points.

👉 INSIDE THE RULE BOOK:

- There are three sets in a bossaball match, and it takes 25 points to win a set.
- In bossaball, any body part can be used to get the ball over the net, including the hands, head, and feet. Each team can have up to eight contacts with the ball on its own side of the court. But players can touch the ball only once with their hands or two times in a row with their feet or head.

Nothing but *Boing!*

slamball:
think basketball
with trampolines

THERE'S ONE SUREFIRE WAY to improve an already perfectly awesome sport. Add a trampoline into the mix! Slamball is a new form of basketball that got its start in California in 2002. It takes place on a springy floor...with the added bonus of four trampolines in front of each net. The trampolines launch players to heights of up to 4.6 m (15 ft.). Like in the NBA (National Basketball Association), players score two points if they sink the ball. But those looking to nab more points launch off the trampoline "slamzones." A basket with that move nets three points. And in case that isn't quite enough action for you, the sport is—oof!—full contact!

At a Glance

There are three positions in slamball:

- **THE HANDLER** sets up plays and tries to keep the opposing team from reaching their basket.

- **THE GUNNER** is the main scorer on the team. This player heads for the trampolines, soaring to the net whenever possible.

- **THE STOPPER** is the team's main defensive player. This player's job is to prevent the opposition from making dunks by slamming into players while in the air.

Teams can choose how they want to arrange their players, but the **usual formations are: one stopper, two handlers, and one gunner, OR one stopper, one handler, and two gunners**.

In slamball, each team can have four players on the court at one time.

the equipment

There's no fooling around in slamball. Even the equipment is serious. Players wear helmets, padded undergarments, and knee and elbow pads. Hmm...wonder why?

dare to compare

A slamball player can bound up to 4.6 m (15 ft.) into the air on a trampoline. Compare that with the heights that these high jumpers of the animal kingdom can reach.

FLEA . . . . 18 cm (7 in.)
SPITTLEBUG . . . . 70 cm (28 in.)
WHITE-TAILED DEER . . 2.6 m (8.5 ft.)
RED KANGAROO . . . . 3 m (10 ft.)
IMPALA . . . . 3.7 m (12 ft.)
PUMA . . . . 5.5 m (18 ft.)
KLIPSPRINGER . . . . . 7.6 m (25 ft.)

47

Calling All Muggles

quidditch: read about Harry Potter's favorite sport or play it. you decide!

IT MAY HAVE BEGUN on the pages of Harry Potter, but the sport of Quidditch has flown into the real world. In fact, it has become a hit at over 300 high schools and colleges around the world. The first official team was formed in 2005 at a college in Vermont. Of course, the muggle version of this sport has had to be altered a bit—especially since genuine Quidditch requires magic and flying. But the object remains the same: score as many goals as possible. Broom's up!

At a Glance

	Number of Players	Pitch (or Field)	Goals	Brooms
QUIDDITCH	seven players on each team	oval-shaped with three hooped goal posts at either end	three ring-shaped goals that float at different levels	players ride magical flying broomsticks
MUGGLE QUIDDITCH	seven players on each team	oval-shaped with three hooped goal posts at either end	hula hoops that are held up at varying heights by plastic pipes	without a jet-powered broomstick, players must carry a broom between their legs

dare to compare

Get a look at the types of balls used in Quidditch.

Quaffle: used to score into one of the three goal hoops. Each score is worth 10 points.

Quidditch: bright-red, hollow ball with four large dimples.	Muggle Quidditch: a slightly deflated volleyball, but a flying disc may be used.

Bludgers: used as an obstacle during game

Quidditch: two iron balls that are bewitched to fly and attempt to hit players off their brooms.	Muggle Quidditch: dodge balls are thrown to knock players off their game.

Golden snitch: used to end and perhaps win the game

Quidditch: a walnut-sized, golden ball. It has silver wings and hovers, darts, and flies around the pitch, avoiding capture.	Muggle Quidditch: a person called the snitch runner who can run outside the playing field— usually dressed in gold; may wear wings.

SPORTS TO SPARE

Could any of these fictitious sports be played in real life?

ANBO-JITSU: Star Trek: The Next Generation
Two players face each other wearing a solid visor, so they can't see a thing. They each use a large stick with a sensor that sends out audio signals, letting each player know the general location of the other.

CALVINBALL: Calvin and Hobbes comic strip
In this sport, the rules are made up on the spot. Scoring ranges from "Q to 12" to "oogy to boogy." Nearly anything goes: a volleyball, a bucket of ice water, a water balloon, and even poetry.

PODRACING: Star Wars: Episode I
This dangerous sport features high-speed one-man vehicles, known as podracers, zipping around a course. Racers were propelled by large turbine engines and could hit speeds of 900 kmh (560 mph).

PYRAMID: Battlestar Galactica
This team-based game takes place on a triangular court, and players can only take three steps at a time. The object of the full-contact sport is to throw a ball through a hole at the top of the pyramid.

People Power

IF YOU'VE EVER BUILT a human pyramid with your friends, you know it can be tricky. But imagine what it takes to build a tower that measures six human stories high! Human tower building, which dates back to the 18th century, occurs at festivals in the Spanish region of Catalonia. Teams compete to create the most elaborate castells, or towers, possible. The bottom of the tower is built slowly, with castellers (that's what you call those who participate in the sport) making a strong base. As the tower gets higher, things move quickly until the final person reaches the top. Then that person climbs down, and the tower begins dismantling.

human tower building: the sport that turns humans into building blocks

SPORT SHORTS

LEAVE IT TO THE PROS!

- The person on the top of the tower is often a kid because of his or her small size and weight.

- The people on the base of a human tower are called the pinya. These team members not only hold the weight of the upper parts of the tower, but they also act as a safety net in case anyone falls down from a higher level.

- A team is not considered to have successfully built a tower until it has been completely dismantled. Castellers come down from the higher levels first until everyone is on the ground safely.

One of the tallest human towers ever featured 150 castellers and stood eight human stories tall.

are you serious?

For an American man named Bryan Berg, it's all in the cards. When he was just eight years old, Berg began building huge structures using only playing cards. At 17, he set the record for the tallest house of cards ever when he built a tower that stood 4.5 m (14.6 ft.) tall. And he recently shattered that record by building a skyscraper that reached a stunning 7.6 m (25 ft.) high!

GOOD BALANCE

NERVES OF STEEL

STRONG

just for laughs

What qualities are needed to be part of a human tower–building team? Let's break it down.

USEFUL TRAITS

Strength
Good Balance
Nerves of Steel

NOT-SO-USEFUL TRAITS

Fear of Heights
Clumsiness
Fear of Crowds

51

And You Thought Road Hockey Was Fun

irish road bowling: sometimes the only place to play is in the streets

YOU CAN FORGET about funky-smelling rental shoes or knocking over pins in this game of bowling. In fact, Irish Road Bowling is more like golf than anything else. The sport, which dates back to the 17th century, is played mainly in Ireland (thus the name!). In this game, players throw an iron ball, called a bullet, down a long and winding country road. And by long, we're talking a distance of up to 4 km (2.5 mi.). The object is to reach the finish line in the fewest throws.

Watch for Traffic

To throw the bullet, the bowler takes a running start and then hurls it underhand. A chalk mark is made on the road wherever the bullet stops, and the next throw is taken from that spot. Of course, since the country lane is not closed to traffic, the bowler must always be alert. A car or truck could show up on the playing course at any time. Beep! Beep!

invention dimension

A Missouri man named Steve Wienecke built a giant pool table in his backyard. He hurls colored bowling balls across the table to play a newfangled game that he calls Knokkers.

SPORT SHORTS

A bowler is usually not alone when he plays Irish Road Bowling. In this case, three's a charm:

- The thrower is the one who hurls the bullet down the country road course.
- The road shower acts like a golf caddy, advising the thrower on how and where to throw the bullet.
- The spotter stands ahead of the thrower and warns of upcoming obstacles, such as cars or potholes.

talk the talk

Before throwing the ball, a player yells:

Faugh an Bheallach!
(say: Fought an ballack)

This Irish phrase means: Clear the way! Since the ball is made of iron, that sounds like good advice.

At a Glance

Get on the ball and look at the differences between Irish Road Bowling and the bowling that most of us are familiar with.

	Ball	Lane	Pins	Shoes	Special Equipment	Hazards
IRISH ROAD BOWLING	small iron ball that's about the size of a tennis ball	long, winding country road that can measure up to 4 km (2.5 mi.) long	no pins	shoe choice is up to the bowler	metal detector to locate ball lost in tall grass or shrubs alongside road	oncoming traffic; injury if hit by the iron ball
BOWLING	hard plastic ball that's about the size of a soccer ball	flat, narrow, and straight lane that extends nearly 19 m (63 ft.)	5 to 10 pins, depending on the game	rubber-soled shoes prevent bowler from sliding on lane	personalized bowling shirt and shoes	nasty foot disease from rental shoes

The Wackiest Sports Stuff Around

There are lots of curious inventions in the world of sports. Here are just a few to pique your interest.

THREE-IN-ONE RIDE

This new mode of getting from here to there is called the Sbyke, and it's part bike, part skateboard, and part scooter. The large front tire lets its rider easily handle even the bumpiest of sidewalks and roads. Let's roll!

PICTURE THIS

Indoor rock walls usually feature small handholds for climbers. But a gym in Japan has decided to make climbers feel more at home. It's created a climbing wall decorated with mirrors, frames, bird cages, and vases. How stylish!

SUMMER SLEDDING

Why wait for winter? The Slicer toboggan lets you hit the slopes even on the warmest of days. This grass-based sled has removable trays on the bottom of it. You fill them with water and place them in the freezer until they turn into blocks of ice. Then you clip the trays back onto the sled and head down the nearest hill.

FOLD, FOLD, FOLD YOUR BOAT

An Israeli designer created this lightweight canoe, which can be folded to fit inside a backpack. The Adhoc Folding Canoe can be assembled in about five minutes, perfect for any on-the-go sailor.

HOP ALONG

Add skipping to the list of activities you can now do on water. The AquaSkipper is a metal-framed contraption that lets you hop across water. It's human-powered, which makes this watercraft enviro-friendly.

I SPY FISH

This contraption takes some of the frustration out of fishing. FishEyes is a fishing rod that has a video camera and monitor attached to it. Both work together to let you see if there are fish in the vicinity of your bait or if it's time to move on to other waters.

THIS OUGHTA BE A HIT

An American company hung several huge punching bags in a subway station in China. Although they were part of an advertisement, the bags were meant to be kicked and punched by commuters. Take that!

IN TUNE

You can crank up the tunes while taking a dip with this MP3 player. The UWater G2 is waterproof, so swimmers can clip the gadget to their goggles and—cannonball!—rock out while doing some laps.

Chapter 3

Off
to the
Races

Think of this page as the starting line and the upcoming section as the *wackiest race track* you'll ever see. With sports that feature *fast-moving* **cheese**, *a sea of rubber* **ducks**, and *high-speed* **woks**, there's no telling what will happen on the way to the finish line. On your mark...*get set*...**read!**

Have Shovel Will Race

SURE, YOU CAN USE A SNOW SHOVEL to clear the driveway for your folks, but that's not nearly as fun as bombing down a hill while sitting on one. In the fast-paced sport of shovel racing, participants sit on a metal shovel and race each other down snowy slopes. This zany activity first hit the powder in the 1970s when ski-lift operators were looking for a quick way to the bottom of the hill. Now every February, the World Snow Shovel Championships are held in New Mexico. This downhill diversion isn't for the faint of heart, though, as speeds can top 110 kmh (70 mph)!

shovel racing: when a shovel is more than a shovel

At a Glance

LEAVE IT TO THE PROS!

Shovel racing is not as simple as sitting on a shovel and burning down a hill. Here's how shovel racers hit the slopes.

STARTING: A racer sits on seat of shovel with handle facing forward between legs. She leans back with her feet off the ground and takes off.

MANEUVERING: To steer, she runs hands in snow. To turn right, racer places right hand in snow. And to turn left, she uses left hand.

STOPPING: Racer drags both hands and feet through snow or lifts up handle so shovel digs into the powder. If all else fails, she bails out!

HERE'S TO HISTORY

Shovel racing hit a snag in 2005 thanks to a version of the sport called modified speed class. In these races, competitors added steering and braking devices to their shovels. While it sounds like a brilliant idea, daredevils ended up creating rides that were so fast they were just plain dangerous. The resort that held shovel races canceled the contests altogether for fear that someone would get injured. But in 2010, the resort had a change of heart. Shovel racers were allowed to return to the slopes on one condition—only unaltered shovels were allowed.

invention dimension

A toboggan that you can wear! You can pull these snow shorts right over your pants for a quick 'n' easy sledding experience. Their padded seat is a built-in sled that lets you fly down the nearest snow-covered hill. And the best part? No dragging a toboggan back up for the next ride!

SPORTS TO SPARE

This is the perfect sport for a couch potato. Every April for 40 years, a resort in Montana celebrated the end of ski season with a big blowout that featured racing furniture down the slopes. People attached skis to couches and other assorted furniture. Then they raced their sweet rides down the mountainside. Judges awarded points for appearance, speed, and accuracy. And the grand prize? A leather recliner, of course!

Take a Wok on the Wild Side

WOKS, THE ROUNDED-BOTTOM pans that have been used for centuries in Asian cooking, have found a new calling...as sports equipment. Believe it or not, this cookware is now being used in a sport known as wok racing. In this pastime, racers sit in a wok and then slide full-speed ahead down an Olympic bobsled run. In fact, there are one-person races and four-person events, where the woks are held together by a wooden frame.

wok racing:
one wok, one icy track,
one to four racers.
mix and hold on tight!

"Wok" This Way

Originally cooked up as a gag by a German entertainer named Stefan Raab, wok racing developed into a genuine sport in 2003 and now the Wok World Championships are held annually. To make sure woks are strong and sport-worthy, the bottoms of the pans have a strong coating called epoxy. And the edges of the pans are covered in a protective sealant to prevent racers from getting injured. As for those wacky—or "wokky"—racers, they can top speeds of 120 kmh (75 mph), so they wear protective gear that's similar to ice hockey equipment.

SPORT SHORTS

What's the best venue for a wok race? These high-speed competitions are held on twisting bobsled tracks. The raceways, which are made of concrete and coated with layers of ice, are about 1,500 m (4,920 ft.) long with drops that can measure 40 stories. There are also plenty of gut-wrenching curves to be had. In fact, racers can feel a force of gravity that measures 5 g—or more than what an astronaut aboard the space shuttle feels during a launch!

great moments in... wok racing

2010
You might think that wok racing is just a flash in the pan, but it has a huge following, especially in Germany. In fact, the Wok World Championships in 2010 drew 6,000 spectators and over 3.5 million people watched the action on television!

the equipment

1. heavy protective gear to prevent injury
2. wok
3. large ladles worn under feet to make for a smooth, faster ride

61

cheese racing: the sport of chasing a wheel of cheese down a steep hill

Where Are My Crackers?

LET'S CUT TO THE CHASE.
The Cooper's Hill Cheese Rolling competition is all about running after a wheel of cheese—yes, cheese—as it rolls down a hill. Sounds simple enough, right? (Even if it is off the charts when it comes to strange.) Well, the race, which is held each year in Gloucester, England, is anything but simple. For starters, the hill is extremely steep. So competitors often end up sliding and somersaulting down its grassy slope. Then there's the fact that catching the cheese is nearly impossible, since it whips along at up to 110 kmh (70 mph). So why does anyone bother with this cheesy challenge? Well, the first person across the finish line wins the cheese. Bonus!

SPORT SHORTS

Cheese rolling isn't all fun and games. The steep and slippery hill has been known to injure a participant or two. In fact, sprained ankles and even broken bones are not uncommon. Then there's that runaway cheese. It moves so quickly that spectators sometimes get knocked over and injured. Guess that explains why first-aid folks are always on hand!

Take this quiz
True or False?

Can you figure out which of these cheese-rolling facts are true and which ones are bogus?

T F **1.** A safety net is set up at the bottom of the hill to prevent the fast-moving cheese from escaping.

T F **2.** The type of cheese that's used in the competition is known as Rolling Romano.

T F **3.** A team of mice is officially released a few minutes before the cheese itself.

T F **4.** There are people at the bottom of the hill to tackle racers who can't slow themselves down at the end of the race.

T F **5.** The competition has been a tradition in Gloucester for at least 200 years.

Answers: 1. True; 2. False. (It's called Double Gloucester); 3. False; 4. True; 5. True (And people come from around the world to participate.)

HERE'S TO HISTORY

This competition hit a bump for a few years. From 1941 to 1954, there were food shortages in England and a big block of cheese wasn't available for the event. Organizers built a wooden wheel instead. A small piece of cheese was placed inside the wooden replica, so the activity could still be called cheese rolling.

just for laughs
It's all cheese, all the time. In 2007, a British cheese maker named Tom Calver set up Cheddarvision, a website that carried live images of a 20 kg (44 lb.) round of cheddar. Visitors to the site could watch the cheese s...l...o...w...l...y age. It may sound like a bore, but the site received nearly one million hits!

are you serious?

In 2006, a group of British cheese makers launched a perfume that smelled like blue Stilton. Hey, who doesn't want to reek like stinky cheese?

All in a Day's Work

YOU'RE IN FOR THE LONG HAUL with these races. They each run nonstop for 24 hours. Talk about motoring morning, noon, and night.

put 24 hours on the clock and let the racing begin

Round and Round We Go

While most go-kart races only include a few laps around the track, endurance karting has its riders hit the blacktop for 24 solid hours. Teams of 2 to 10 drivers take turns going full-out in the karts. But riders don't have to show up with their own personal go-karts. For these competitions, karts, mechanics, and even fuel are all provided.

Keep Rolling

The 24hrs Inline Montreal relay race attracts over a thousand skaters from around the world. Teams of up to 10 in-line skaters try to complete as many laps as possible around the 4.7 km (2.9 mi.) course within 24 hours. The race is a relay, so racers must pass a baton before another team member can skate around the course.

Start Your Engines...and Keep Them Going and Going

The 24 Hours of Le Mans car race has been held each June in the French town of Le Mans since 1923. During the day-long drivefest, teams of three share a race car, and each member spends about two hours behind the wheel. On their break, drivers snag some food and catch a bit of shut-eye until it's time to take over driving duties again. Each team travels up to 5,000 km (3,105 mi.) over the 24 hours of racing.

Now That's a Bike Ride

The 24-Hours of Adrenalin mountain bike event takes place in North America each year in locations including Alberta, California, and Georgia. Solo riders or teams of up to 10 people ride their mountain bikes along a designated course for as many laps as possible over a 24-hour period. That means racing in the dead of night with only a headlamp to light the way. The biker who travels the most laps receives a jersey and a medal.

Make a Run for It

It's called an ultramarathon for a reason. This type of 24-hour run involves a competitor running as far as he or she can in a 24-hour span. Runners sprint around a track or a short road course over and over (and over) again, typically running about 210 km (130 mi.) before the day is done. And get this: the world record for a 24-hour run belongs to a German man named Yiannis Kouros who ran nearly 304 km (189 mi.) on a track in Australia in 1997.

⚛ the science spot

Take a look at a day in the life of YOU by finding out what happens to the average person during a 24-hour period.

Number of times you laugh.....................adults 17; kids 300–400
Number of times you blink...........................17,000
Number of times you take a breath.............21,000
Number of times your heart beats 96,000
Number of skin cells you shed:... almost one million
Number of hairs you lose............................ 50–100
Number of words you say 16,000
Length your nails grow...............1 mm (0.0039 in.)
Length your hair grows ....44 mm (0.017 in.)

Burning up the Blacktop

IT TAKES A NEED FOR SPEED and a stomach full of guts to tackle street luging. After all, participants lie flat on a wheeled sled that's just inches from the ground and burn down a paved course at breakneck speeds... with no brakes in sight. Street luge got its start in southern California in the 1970s when skateboarders found they could go faster by lying on their boards. Racers soon upgraded to longer boards and began racing professionally. Today, brave lugers battle to be the first to cross the finish line in races around the world, including at the annual Street Luge World Cup.

street luging: you'd better have a bowlful of courage for breakfast before trying this sport

All A-Board

Street luge races are usually held on mountain roads with bales of hay alongside the course to cushion racers who wipe out. The racing technique is pretty simple. Racers lie on their backs with their toes pointed forward and their bodies as flat as possible. Then they hold on for dear life! Steering is done by carefully leaning from side to side. And with no braking system in place (whose idea was that?), racers must drag their feet along the ground to stop or slow down. Some racers add tire treads to the outside of their shoes so that they don't burn up as they're dragged along the blacktop.

At a Glance

LEAVE IT TO THE PROS!

Here's how street lugers roll with it:

STARTING: Riders push off using their hands. This is the only time that hands can be used, with the exception of when a racer needs to start rolling again after a crash.

MANEUVERING: To change position as they're racing, lugers shift their weight from side to side.

STOPPING: While racers usually drag their feet to stop, they may choose to slow themselves down by sitting upright. This increases wind resistance and helps to reduce their speed gradually.

talk the talk

BACON: has nothing to do with breakfast. This term refers to rough and dangerous road conditions.

BANANA: describes a rider who wipes out a lot. (Guess they slip up!)

DROP A HILL: means riding a luge course

HYSTERIA: means it might be time to panic—an uncontrolled wobble during a race that usually results in a wipeout

SCRAMBLED EGGS: again, nothing to do with breakfast. It's the term for a bad road surface. But it's not as bad as "bacon."

SPEED WOBBLES: sounds like a toy but is actually uncontrollable wobbling during a race. It's also called "wobbs."

WAIL OR WAILING: used to describe a luger who's going "wicked" fast

are you serious?

Why bother with a board? In 1994, a French designer named Jean-Yves Blondeau developed a 31-wheel roller suit that takes high-speed fun to another level entirely. The suit places wheels under just about every part of Blondeau's body and allows him to roll along at speeds of up to 110 kmh (70 mph). Sounds "wheely" fun!

Release the Ducks!

rubber duck race: why should humans have all the fun?

THOSE SOFT AND SQUISHY rubber ducks that bob in bathtubs are now part of races held in places like Canada, England, and Singapore. In these competitions, hundreds and sometimes thousands of rubber ducks are dumped into a river. From there, the little quackers float down a marked race course. The first one to cross the finish line is victorious. The ducks are typically "adopted" by individuals, and the winning duck's owner often collects prize money. To keep the races enviro-friendly, the rubber ducks are then "rescued" from the water to be used in a future race.

RECORD BREAKER!

It's safe to say that Charlotte Lee likes rubber ducks. This American woman has a record-breaking collection of the yellow bath toys. Since 1996, she has amassed over 5,600 unique rubber ducks. And her collection just keeps growing. How quack-tacular!

great moments in...
rubber duck racing

2009

A rubber duck race in London, England, set a world record when 205,000 blue plastic ducks were set free on the river Thames. The winning duck netted its owner $20,000 US. Now that's a lot of ducks!

2011

A duck race that was held in Queensland, Australia, featured a motorized rubber duck derby. For the race, large rubber ducks captained toy speedboats. They puttered along trying to nab the fastest motorized duck award.

are you serious?

If your bathtime toys are a bit blah, here's one that might catch your soapy eye. This top-of-the-line rubber duck is covered in 5,000 crystals. But its cost might sink your spirits, since it rings in at a whopping $1,000 US!

the science spot

In January of 1992, about 29,000 bath toys, including rubber ducks, were washed off a ship sailing in the Pacific Ocean. Since that time, they've floated halfway around the world on ocean currents and continue to wash up on the shores of Canada, the United States, Australia, and South America. Funnily enough, an oceanographer named Curtis Ebbesmeyer actually tracks the movements of the runaway ducks, helping us learn more about ocean currents.

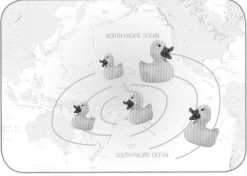

Who Needs Water?

THE HENLEY-ON-TODD REGATTA is unlike any other boat race in the world. What sets it apart? It's held on land! Named after Henley-on-Thames, England, the site of the Henley Royal Regatta rowing race, it takes place on the sandy bed of the Todd River, in Alice Springs, Australia. This contest has been held every August for more than 50 years. Teams of "rowers" run in bottomless "boats" along the hot sand, racing toward a buoy and then back to the finish line. Even if they wanted to race on water, they couldn't. The nearest large body of water is 1,500 km (932 mi.) away.

henley-on-todd regatta: the only river race where water is not required

There are several types of races that are part of the fun during the Henley-on-Todd Regatta. Sail in for a look!

BRING YOUR OWN BOAT: Teams design a boat. A crew of four must race it along the sandy bed of the Todd River.

MAXI-YACHT: A crew of 8 to 10 runs along the sandy course in a large, bottomless yacht.

BATHTUB DERBY: Four racers carry a teammate in a bathtub. Midway through the race, they must pour a bucket of water into the tub and then carry it back to the finish line.

BOOGIE BOARD: Five teammates make their way through the sandy course, pulling another team member who's standing or kneeling on a "surfboard."

SAND SKIS: Four team members strap "water skis" to their feet and try to ski their way along the sand to the finish line.

BATTLE BOAT SPECTACULAR: For the race's last day, three trucks that are decked out like boats drive through the sand. They blast flour bombs and water cannons at racers and spectators alike.

great moments in...
henley-on-todd regatta

1993

One of the most ridiculous moments in the race's history came in 1993. The boat race had to be canceled due to flooding when wet weather filled the river with water. Imagine that!

are you serious?

From boats on land to cars in the water. Meet the Python, an amphibious vehicle that transforms from a car into a boat. To ditch dry land, a driver shifts into boat mode and pushes a button to lift the wheels. Then it's clear sailing. The five-seater can even reach highway speeds on the water. It's the ultimate transformer!

the science spot

HOW IS SAND FORMED? Sand is created when rocks are slowly worn down over thousands of years by wind, rain, and other forces. Eventually, only tiny grains of sand remain. The loose grains are eventually picked up by wind and water and deposited in the ocean or as sand dunes on land.

SAND SONGS Believe it or not, there is sand that sounds like it's singing. Scientists think it has something to do with the way that wind passes over it. The sand must also have specific qualities to sing: grains must be round and damp, and contain a mineral called silica. Other sand sounds that have been heard include whistling, barking, squeaking, and roaring.

On your Mark, Get Set... Go!

IT'S OFF TO THE RACES for a look at some of the wackier racing competitions around.

Baa, Baa, Black Sheep, I'll Carry Your Wool

You can always have a race up a steep road. But why not make it interesting and carry sacks of wool enroute? The Tetbury Woolsack Races, which are held each year in Gloucestershire, England, feature racers carrying heavy sacks of wool on their backs as they race along a course.

Sleep on It

When you snooze, you lose. That's especially true in the Amazing Bed Race. This competition is held in Burlington, Ontario, every September. Competitors build a bed, decorate it, and then race along a course. The bed must have four wheels and no motor. Teams are made up of four pushers and one rider, who must sit on the bed at all times.

Don't Stop to Shop

We're used to seeing them stuffed with groceries, but shopping carts are now a vehicle of choice for some racers. Shopping cart races take place around the United States, with New York, Chicago, and San Francisco leading the charge. Teams of five tie themselves to a cart and are given basic race information. While they all have the same start and finish lines, the teams are free to choose their own route.

If the shoe hurts, run in it

Who needs sneakers? To compete in New York City's annual High Heel-A-Thon race, women—and a few daring men—wear high heels in the 150-meter dash. The first one to sprint across the finish line is a shoe-in for the $25,000 US prize and also runs away with a shoe-shaped trophy.

don't go anywhere

You can now win a bike race without ever leaving home. Sound impossible? Ride into the world of stationary bike racing. A new bicycle called the Ergo Bike allows riders to race each other virtually. They just pick a time and a virtual course to compete in a head-to-head race with another biker.

BRING ON THE BATHTUBS

For nearly 30 years, the International Regatta of Bathtubs has been held on a river in Belgium. This madcap race features nonmotorized watercrafts that must be constructed with at least one bathtub. Over 20,000 spectators flock to the riverbanks to watch!

The Tale of the Snail

Every year in Norfolk, England, snails take center stage at the World Snail Racing Championships. These slowpokes are placed in the middle of a circular track. A referee yells, "Ready, steady, slow!" And they're off. Sort of...

when you gotta go...

The Outhouse Races in Trenary, Michigan, have been held every February since 1994. This competition features teams pushing homemade outhouses on skis down the town's snowy main street.

high-speed sitter

Office chair racing began in Germany in 2008. Contestants bring an office chair to the downhill race course, take a seat, and get rolling. Besides reaching speeds of up to 35 kmh (22 mph), racers have to deal with ramps and jumps along the way.

73

It's Potty Time

WHEN IT COMES TO THESE COMPETITIONS, you really gotta go. Toilet bowl races feature two competitors battling to the finish line while seated on...take a guess. The toilets that are used in these unusual races, which take place mainly in the United States, are a far cry from the porcelain fixtures you find behind closed doors. These have been modified to make them race-ready. Competitors bolt the toilets to a base with wheels or to a large tricycle. They climb aboard their ride at the starting line atop a hill. And with a push from a teammate, the racers are on a roll. They weave their way down the hill until they thump into hay bales that are lined up to stop them at the bottom of the course.

toilet bowl races: proof that you can race just about anything

Let's Motor

In some toilet races, there's no hill to be had. Instead, racers sit atop their portable toilets and are pushed around a course by teammates. And then there's the next level of toilet bowl racing. In this version of the sport, racers ride motorized toilets. They swerve around cones on their electric-powered rides in an effort to be the fastest one around the course.

When you're talking about fast-moving toilets, you simply can't ignore this invention by a British man named Edd China (opposite page). This motor specialist created the world's fastest toilet. The motorized toilet has sink handlebars and a bathtub for a sidecar. And the record-breaking ride has a top speed of 68 kmh (42 mph).

Take this quiz
True or Flush?

T F 1. Historians believe one of the earliest toilets was used in Scotland back in 3000 BC.

T F 2. In the 15th century, people used a special metal or ceramic bowl as a toilet and often threw its contents out the window.

T F 3. The first flush toilet was invented in 1804 and was built for the French Emperor Napoléon.

T F 4. The average person uses a toilet 2,500 times per year.

T F 5. An Australian company has designed a toilet that can be used by four people at the same time.

T F 6. The first toilet used in space came equipped with a lap belt.

Answers: 1. True; 2. True; 3. False. (It was invented in 1596 for Queen Elizabeth I.); 4. True; 5. False; 6. True

Putting the "Y" in YUK

Normally, a bathroom is the last room in the house where you'd take your food. Not so at the Chinese restaurant chain called Modern Toilet. At these eateries, customers sit on toilet chairs (lids down, of course!), dine at glass-topped bathtub tables, and eat from toilet-shaped bowls!

are you serious?

We're guessing this toilet won't get a lot of use. For starters, it's gold-plated, and then there's the fact that it's worth about $250,000 US! The posh potty, unveiled in November 2011 at the World Toilet Summit and Expo, is ceramic at its core and coated with a thick layer of 24-karat gold.

 invention dimension

It's usually not a good thing when a goldfish ends up in the vicinity of a toilet. But that's not the case with the Fish 'n' Flush aquarium. This fishy fixture turns a toilet into a home for your favorite swimmer. The toilet's tank has two pieces—one is a fill tank for the toilet and the other is the actual aquarium. And while it may look like the little fishies in the tank could head for the sewer system at any time, the fact is they're never in danger of being flushed.

The Shear Fun of It

YOU COULD SAY THIS SPORT is a cut above the rest. In the land of lawn mower racing, competitors climb aboard ride-on mowers and tool around a dirt track, trying to be the first to cross the finish line. And the racers really go full out, topping speeds of up to 95 kmh (60 mph). Of course, the mowers have had their blades removed for safety's sake. This cutting edge sport started small in 1973. But today, it has grown to have leagues in England, the United States, and Australia. In fact, races are known to attract a few thousand spectators. Ready, set, mow!

lawn mower racing: one part lawn mower, no part cutting grass

👉 INSIDE THE RULE BOOK:

While lawn mower racing may seem like an easygoing sport, there are certainly rules to mow by:

1. Drivers must be 18 years old to participate. But anyone from 8 to 17 can enter a race if they get their parent's go-ahead. Pass the permission form!

2. All lawn mowers must be designed to mow lawns.

3. Blades must be removed from all racing lawn mowers. (Sharp idea.)

4. All mowers must have working brakes... because having the ability to stop is always useful.

5. While on the track, every driver must wear a safety helmet, a neck support, long pants, a long-sleeved shirt, and gloves. Off the track, fashion choices are all up to you.

✳ Take this quiz

Lawn mower racers come up with some of the wackiest names for their rides. See if you can guess which of these unusual names are the real deal.

1. SODZILLA
2. GERONIMOW
3. ABOMINABLE MOWMAN
4. TURFINATOR
5. MOWTER MANIA
6. THE GREAT GRASSHOPPER
7. BATMOWBILE

Answers: 1. Real; 2. Real; 3. Fake; 4. Real; 5. Fake; 6. Fake; 7. Real

💡 invention dimension

Sheep love to munch on grass. So it's no wonder that a professor at a Pennsylvania university invented a lawn mower that looks like the wooly farm animal. Called the Mower, this robotic sheep scurries along on six little legs, cutting the grass with its lawn-mowing teeth. Chomp!

are you serious?

Turns out you don't need paint to create a museum-worthy masterpiece. A British man found that a small lawn mower and a variety of garden tools will do the job just fine. In July of 2008, artist Chris Naylor used grass-trimming gear to turn a lawn in London, England, into a replica of Leonardo da Vinci's Mona Lisa. The creative clipping took Naylor two days to complete and grew out in a few weeks.

Extreme Sports Venues

Sometimes it's not so much the sport that's unusual, but the place where it's played. Have a look at these off-the-wall sporty spots.

ROLLING ON A ROLLER COASTER

On a good day, a roller coaster can give your nerves a jolt. But a German in-line skater decided to take it up a notch. In the summer of 2009, Dirk Auer in-line skated down a roller coaster, topping out at speeds of 90 kmh (56 mph). Auer wore specially designed skates that fit onto the coaster's rails. The daredevil completed the gut-turning run in just over a minute. Whoosh!

TENNIS, ANYONE?

This tennis court takes things to new heights. In February 2005, a helipad high atop a hotel in Dubai was temporarily transformed into a grass tennis court. About 213 m (700 ft.) above the ground, tennis stars Andre Agassi and Roger Federer played a friendly match. Bet they had a ball!

GET SQUASHED

Catch a train and...a game of squash? For the past 15 years, a squash tournament has been held in New York City's Grand Central Terminal, a major train station in the city. The action takes place in a glass-enclosed squash court, which is set up smack-dab in the midst of the station's hustle and bustle. There's even seating for spectators.

RAD RAMP

You'll get wicked air on this skateboard ramp...and maybe a touch of air sickness, too. The ridiculously huge Mega Ramp is found in San Diego, California. This wooden structure is longer than a football field. Plus, it stands as tall as an eight-storey building, allowing boarders to plummet down its incline at speeds topping 90 kmh (55 mph). How sick!

GET THE DRIFT

When did soccer become a water sport? This field in Singapore is actually a floating platform for sports matches, as well as concerts and other events. The Float at Marina Bay can hold up to 1,070 tonnes, which is about the weight of 9,000 people. As for spectators, they have to settle for watching from land. There's a gallery alongside the field that holds up to 30,000 people.

YOUR THRONE AWAITS

There's no question that sitting in box seats at a sporting event is the ultimate. But imagine watching a game from a fifteenth-century castle! A soccer field in Croatia has a stone palace sitting directly alongside it, so spectators can behave like royalty and take in a game from the regal structure.

GO, GREEN, GO

The Janguito Malucelli in Brazil is eco-friendly. No concrete was used during its construction, as designers chose to use reclaimed wood instead. Plus, the seats for the 6,000 spectators who come to watch soccer were built individually into a grassy hillside.

OUT TO SEA

Soccer could get soggy at this stadium. The soccer pitch in the Faeroe Islands—halfway between Scotland and Iceland—sits at the edge of the Norwegian Sea. In fact, with the water so close by, there's always a boat on call to fish out any soccer balls that head for the deep.

IT'S ONLY NATURAL

This new stadium in Shenzhen, China, was inspired by the forests found in the southern part of the country. That's why the exterior of the building is surrounded by large, green, steel poles that look just like bamboo. The poles aren't just for looks, though. They provide structural support for the roof of the Bao'an Stadium.

Chapter 4

Wet, Wild & Weird Water Sports

You can file these sports under H for **"huh."** There's something not quite right about *hauling a bike* to the bottom of the ocean. Or *sailing the seas* in a **pumpkin**. But that's just why these pastimes are sure to make a **splash** on the sports scene.

Bogged Down

SNORKEL—CHECK. FLIPPERS—CHECK. Muddy, cold, water-filled trench—check. Dive in to the sport of bog snorkeling. Held each year in Wales, the World Bog Snorkelling Championships dare competitors to swim two laps through a 1.8 m (6 ft.) deep trench that's oozing with murky swamp water. The person to complete the filthy challenge in the fastest time is the champ. But to make things a little bit tougher, no proper swimming strokes are allowed. That means swimmers who take to the sludge must rely on flipper-power only.

bog snorkeling: a sport for those who think swimming in swamp water sounds like a day at the beach

the science spot

What is a bog? This soggy spot is a wetland that's made up of dead plant materials, quite often mosses. And the water that flows out of bogs is usually a lovely shade of brown. Bogs are found in cool climates, the largest one being in Russia's Western Siberian Lowlands. It covers more than 600,000 square kilometers (372,823 sq. mi.).

SPORTS TO SPARE

For those who find bog snorkeling lacks a little something, there's always the Bog Snorkeling Triathlon. This event, which first took place in 2005, begins with a 12 km (7.5 mi.) run, followed by two lengths in the bog trench, and is topped off with a 30 km (19 mi.) mountain bike ride on some seriously rugged terrain. That'll get your heart pumping!

great moments in... bog snorkeling

1995 Believe it or not, the World Bog Snorkelling Championships had to be canceled in 1995 due to a drought. Guess you can't snorkel in a bog when there is no bog!

are you serious?

Check out another twist on snorkeling. Helmet diving is a deep-sea activity that allows people to head into the underwater world safely...all while looking rather, um, unique. A diving helmet is placed over your head, so it rests on your shoulders. Once it's in place, you can breathe normally thanks to long air lines that pump oxygen into the helmet. Explore away!

83

Watered Down Fun

THIS EVENT GIVES A WHOLE new meaning to the term "sinking a putt." Back in 2007, the first ever underwater golf tournament was held in an aquarium in China. Five golfers grabbed golf clubs, strapped on scuba gear, and dove to the bottom of a 15 m (50 ft.) tank for the moist matchup. Unlike the land version of the sport, a winner was not determined by who had the least number of shots. It came down to who could get the ball into the hole in the shortest amount of time.

underwater golf: sink or swim. or practice your golf swing

I've Got a Sinking Feeling

As you might imagine, golfers face unique challenges while playing on an underwater course. For starters, fish and turtles swimming nearby are a constant distraction during the game. Plus, the water currents change the golf ball's direction without a moment's notice, making it pretty near impossible for golfers to predict where their ball will go next. Guess they just have to go with the flow!

SPORTS TO SPARE

This isn't exactly underwater, but it's pretty close. A floating golf course is under development in the Maldives, an island off the coast of India. The golf hot spot, which is due to be completed in 2015, will have 18 holes spread out over three separate floating platforms. Golfers will walk through clear, underwater tunnels to move between the platforms, giving them the chance to take in marine life as they play.

Take this quiz

Take a swing at trying to figure out the meaning of these golfing terms by unscrambling the words.

1. ETE FOF	To hit a ball from the ground at the start of a hole
2. NGERE	Officially, it's the whole golf course
3. REOF	What players yell to warn others they're hitting the ball
4. AIRFWYA	The part of a course between the tee and the putting green
5. EAC	A hole in one
6. ADZHRA	Any spot that's an obstacle, such as a sand trap or lake
7. VOTDI	A piece of grass that's torn out by a golf club
8. ARP	The number of strokes normally needed for a certain hole

Answers: 1. Tee off; 2. Green; 3. Fore; 4. Fairway; 5. Ace; 6. Hazard; 7. Divot; 8. Par

are you serious?

Golfers need a boat to tackle the 14th hole at a golf course in Idaho. The Coeur d'Alene Resort Golf Course is home to the world's only floating putting green. Once you hit your ball to the island that's drifting just offshore, you have to board a shuttle boat to complete the hole.

invention dimension

You hit a golf ball and it sails through the sky...straight into a cluster of shrubs growing alongside the green. Instead of going on a wild-goose chase looking for your lost ball, you could track it down with a gadget called the RadarGolf System. This system comes complete with golf balls that have a microchip embedded in their core. A handheld tracking device picks up a signal coming from the ball, so you can easily find it. It's high-tech hide-and-seek!

Soaking Cycle

IF YOU TOLD YOUR FOLKS you were taking your bike for a spin on the bottom of the Atlantic, they'd probably take away your biking privileges for good. But every July, water-loving bikers in North Carolina do just that. It's all part of the Discovery Diving Underwater Bike Race. To get started, a boat takes cyclists about 30 minutes offshore to the race site. Then bikes are dropped into the water. The cyclists, who are dressed in scuba gear, quickly leap into the sea, grab a bike, and head 18 m (60 ft.) below the surface.

underwater bike race: cycling on dry land is so yesterday

Sink 'n' Cycle

The race itself is held alongside a 98 m (320 ft.) long sunken ship that now serves as an artificial reef on the ocean floor. Once in the deep, racers start the tough task of cycling the entire length of the shipwreck. That means doing whatever it takes, including swimming, dragging, or pushing their bike. Typically, the race takes about 15 minutes. And spectators are welcome to cheer on the racers. They can view the action from the charter boat that brings everyone to the site or scuba dive for a fish-eye view!

 invention dimension

just for laughs

What You Need for Underwater Biking: *scuba tank, wetsuit, goggles, flippers, old bike*

What You Don't Need: *bike helmet, running shoes, water bottle, horn or bell*

You'll need a life jacket for this bike. The Shuttle Bike lets you ride on the water. This wet 'n' wild invention transforms a regular mountain bike into a floating water-bicycle in just 10 minutes. Better yet, everything you need to complete the transformation fits inside a backpack. To make the Shuttle Bike, you first clamp a metal frame to your bicycle. Then you pump up a pair of long, yellow floats and attach them to the frame. Once on the water, a propeller moves the bike forward as you pedal. Ride those waves!

are you serious?

If you're looking for an underwater bike ride without all that pesky pedaling, the Scuba-Doo motorized bike may be just for you. This aquatic cycle has a breathing dome that fits over your head and shoulders. The sweet ride can carry enough air in its tanks to keep you breathing for an hour-long bike ride in the deep. Just "doo" it.

In July 2008, an Italian man named Vittorio Innocente pedaled into the record books by completing the deepest underwater bike ride. Innocente, who was decked out in scuba gear, was lowered into the Mediterranean Sea by a team of divers. The record-breaking biker then rode at a depth of 65 m (214 ft.), smashing a record that he'd set three years earlier. To succeed at these deep-sea outings, Innocente doesn't ride any ordinary bike. He attaches water-filled tires and weights to his mountain bike to make it heavier so that it doesn't float.

Travel the World

around the world yacht race: the perfect sport for anyone looking to get in touch with their inner Christopher Columbus

GOT A YEAR TO SPARE? Then you may want to get on board with the Clipper Round the World Yacht Race. In this adventurous event, 10 yachts race around the globe for 11 months, making it the world's longest sailing race. The competition was created in 1996 by Sir Robin Knox-Johnston, a British man who was the first person to sail solo and nonstop around the world. Today, 10 yachts hit the high seas for an eight-leg, 64,375 km (40,000 mi.) race around the world.

All Hands on Deck

So what does it take to get a spot on one of these 21 m (68 ft.) racing yachts? No experience is necessary! In fact, the crew members on all the yachts are amateur sailors. That said, each team does have one experienced skipper to captain and oversee things. (Smart thinking!) Teams are awarded points at the end of each leg, based on their position and the condition of the ship and its sails. In the end, the team with the most points sails off with the Clipper Trophy. Take a bow!

At a Glance

The route that yachts take for the Clipper Round the World Yacht Race changes each year. To see how crew members circle the globe, check out this example of the route from the race's 15th anniversary year.

talk the talk

Learn the language of sailing with these seafaring terms:

STARBOARD: the right side of a boat

PORT: the left side of a boat

BOW: the front section of a boat

STERN: the rear section of a boat

HULL: a boat's frame or body

GALLEY: the kitchen

HEADS: the toilets

WINCH: a lifting device used for hoisting ropes

VERTICAL SPARS: the upright masts used to support rigging and sails

HORIZONTAL SPARS OR BOOMS: the masts that lie across the boat and hold the sails

SPORT SHORTS

Before you get all Captain Jack Sparrow and apply to join the Clipper Yacht Race, you should consider the work that's required. First off, training isn't an option. This race is serious business, so sailors must be prepared before heading out to sea. Crew members learn everything from sailing skills and sea safety to navigation and meteorology. Plus, each crew member works in every position on the boat, which means taking on the role of chef, plumber, sail repairer, and so on. It's definitely not a relaxing day (or year) at sea!

the science spot

You're sailing on the open sea when suddenly your stomach starts to churn. Every movement of the boat makes you a little queasier. And then...yup...here comes your lunch. So just what causes sea sickness? Your brain collects data from your eyes, ears, and the rest of your body to figure out what you're doing at any given moment. When you're on a boat, your inner ears sense the motion, so they tell your brain that you're moving. But your eyes see that everything around you on the boat itself is motionless. Your brain starts getting mixed messages. And when things don't make sense...stand back!

Roaring down the Rapids

THE WATER RUSHES AROUND YOU as you maneuver through the roaring rapids. All the while, you cling to the one thing keeping you afloat—a small foam board. But you're not afraid. In fact, you're having the time of your life. That's the power of riverboarding, a thrilling white-water sport that finds participants storming down rapids while lying stomach-first on a riverboard. The key to this board sport is a pair of flippers. They help boarders steer and propel themselves through the rapids.

riverboarding: the best way to get a face full of rapids

dare to compare

Riverboarders travel down class 4 or 5 rapids. Hit the surf for a rundown of the different classes of rapids.

Class 1: Slow-moving river with gentle curves and no rough areas.

Class 2: Has some rough water and may require a bit of maneuvering around rocks. It's suitable for beginners.

Class 3: Has a faster moving current and numerous high and irregular white-water waves.

Class 4: Water is fast-moving and has large waves, rocks, and some significant drops. You should have white-water experience to tackle these rapids.

Class 5: Large, turbulent waves, strong currents, big rocks, and some significant drops. These rapids are extremely difficult to maneuver, so you need to have white-water experience.

Class 6: Huge waves, rocks, and drops. These rapids are regarded as hazardous even for those considered experts.

SPORTS TO SPARE

Today riverboarding is a hit in New Zealand and Europe. But this go-with-the-flow sport got its start in the French Alps during the 1970s. Legend has it that local raft guides were looking for a more adventurous way to cruise down rivers. So they tied life jackets together, held on tightly, and blasted down the surf. Eventually, they used foam boards for a more stable ride, and a sport was born!

For those who want to hit the rapids in a little more comfort, river bugging may be the way to flow. This water sport, which hit the waves of New Zealand in 1997, features a one-person raft that resembles an inflatable chair. Riders sit in their river bug and race down rapids. And since there's no paddle, participants wear webbed gloves and short flippers while "bugging."

Also known as hydrospeed in Europe and white-water sledging in New Zealand

surf's up

Normally surfers head to sea to catch gnarly waves. But, since the 1970s, many athletes swear by river surfing. In fact, in some places, these surfers can spend the day surfing just one wave. Called a standing wave, it never goes away thanks to a constant surge of water coming from over a rock. In these cases, surfers face upstream and catch the wave. While they feel like they're being carried along by the rush of water, they're actually not moving downstream at all.

Paddle that Pumpkin

WHY CARVE A PUMPKIN into a jack-o'-lantern when you can turn it into a mode of transportation instead? At the Pumpkin Paddling Regatta that's held every October in Windsor, Nova Scotia, racers sail across a lake in monster-sized gourds. For the competition, which got growing in 1999, hundreds of locals spend the days before the big event hollowing out giant pumpkins that weigh about 272 kg (600 lb.). On the big day, racers climb into the cockpit of their PVCs—that's personal vegetable crafts—and start paddling.

pumpkin racing: the only way to combine veggies with a sport...so far

3.14

The Race Is On

A crowd of about 10,000 people cheer on the paddle-powered pumpkins as they travel the 800 m (.5 mi.) course. Some pumpkin boats just aren't up to the challenge and end up sinking like a stone. But the racer whose watercraft manages to stay afloat and crosses the finish line first takes home a carved wooden pumpkin trophy. **Victory!**

the equipment

Where do they find those huge pumpkins anyway? It just so happens that Windsor, Nova Scotia, is home to some of the biggest pumpkins on the planet. A local pumpkin grower named Howard Dill developed the Atlantic Giant in the 1970s. These eye-catching pumpkins are so gigantic that you can carve them into, well, a boat!

are you serious?

Your parents may hound you about eating your veggies. But what do you think they'd say about playing them instead? A 12-member orchestra from Vienna uses instruments made from pumpkins and other vegetables during their performances. The First Vienna Vegetable Orchestra plays concerts using pumpkin drums, carrot flutes, and bell pepper trumpets. The group carves the instruments before each concert, and sometimes audiences are offered vegetable soup made from the instruments after the show!

SPORT SHORTS

While the paddling event is the most popular race of the day at the Pumpkin Regatta, there is a motorized event that attracts a dozen competitors or so. Yes, that's right. Racers in this contest attach a motor to their pumpkin and putter their way to the finish line.

SPORTS TO SPARE

If pumpkins can float, then surely they can fly, too!? In the sport of pumpkin chunking—yes, that is an actual sport—people hurl pumpkins through the sky using machines that work like huge slingshots and catapults. There's even an event called the World Championship Punkin Chunkin contest that's held each November. Over 100 teams compete to fire their pumpkin the farthest. Amazingly, some pumpkins fly over 915 m (3,000 ft.)—or about as far as 130 school buses parked end to end!

great moments in... pumpkin racing

Nova Scotian Leo Swinamer was an expert at leaving the competition behind at the Pumpkin Paddling Competition. He won the first nine—count 'em, nine—years of the contest before retiring. Swinamer took the races very seriously, growing the pumpkins himself and carefully carving his veggie ride until it was just right.

A Stone's Throw

stone skipping: there's no denying it, this sport rocks

YOU FIND A SMALL, FLAT ROCK BESIDE A LAKE and flick it across the water's surface. Skip...skip... skip...plop. Skipping rocks is a pastime all over the world. In fact, Inuit even skip rocks on ice! But in some places, this carefree activity has turned into a serious competition. For instance, on Mackinac Island in Michigan, an annual stone skipping tournament has been making a splash for over 45 years. Competitors from across the United States test their skipping skills, with some skipping rocks across the water's surface over 30 times.

How to...Skip Stones

What's the best way to get a stone to skip over the water? Russell Byars—stone skipper extraordinaire—shares these tips to perfect your technique.

1. Find a wave-free lake or river. Look for a thin, flat rock that weighs about as much as a golf ball.

2. Hold the stone with your index finger and thumb, forming the shape of the letter "C." The rock can rest on your other fingers for support.

3. Face the water at a bit of an angle. Stay crouched low to the ground because the stone needs to be as parallel to the water's surface as possible.

4. As you throw the rock, snap your wrist to give it some spin. Follow through by swinging your arm and use your index finger to push the rock off.

5. Keep practicing and adjust the speed and spin of your throws to become the ultimate stone skipper.

TIP: Never throw rocks where people are swimming

are you serious?

It has baffled scientists for decades. Large rocks in a California desert move across the sand on their own, leaving behind long trails. Over the course of a year, one rock can travel more than 320 m (1,050 ft.) across the flat, dried-up lake bed. Since the area is so remote, no one really knows how it happens, but there is one theory. As the temperature drops at night, a thin layer of ice forms on the rocks. Then, when strong winds blow, the stones are slowly nudged across the sand. Mystery solved?

the science spot

So why does a stone actually skip? It comes down to four key things: the rock itself, some spin, some speed, and the perfect angle.

* flat, thin, round rocks have a surface that allows them to skip smoothly across the water

* the spinning of a stone keeps it from plummeting to the bottom of a lake or river when it hits the water's surface

* a steady speed also makes sure the rock doesn't sink like, well, a stone before it has a chance to skip

* experts have determined that for optimum skipping, you need an angle of about 20 degrees between a stone and the water

talk the talk

It's commonly known as stone skipping or stone skimming. But here's what it's called in a few other places around the globe.

In England: ducks and drakes
In Denmark: smutting
In France: ricochet
In Ireland: stone skiffing

great moments in... stone skipping

2007 What a throw! In July 2007, an American man named Russell Byars skipped a rock an astonishing 51 times across a river in Pennsylvania.

95

Make a Splash

WHEN OLYMPIC DIVERS HIT THE WATER, they try to make their entry as clean as possible. That means the less splash the better. With splashdiving, it's the exact opposite. This sport is all about the splash. In fact, the object is to make the biggest splash you can. The main event for this sport is the Splashdiving World Championship that's held in Hamburg, Germany. Divers climb up to a platform that's 10 m (33 ft.) high. Without a sliver of fear, they leap and smack down hard on the water. And anything goes, including belly flops and back-first landings. Um...ow.

splashdiving: a sport where the biggest splash reigns supreme

How to...
Do the Perfect Cannonball

Here's the inside scoop on how to make the most of your splash. (Tip: Don't attempt a cannonball if you cannot swim. And always be sure that you're supervised by an adult.)

1. Make sure water is much deeper than your height. And pool should be clear of swimmers.

2. Take a few steps back from edge of pool. Step forward quickly and jump out and over water as high as possible—and away from edge of pool.

3. Scream "Cannonball!" at top of your lungs.

4. Make tight ball by holding knees to chest. Tuck in chin.

5. Hold breath.

invention dimension

If you usually need a little push before you're ready to take a dip, here it is. An invention called the AirKick is a catapult that launches you into a swimming pool. The rider sits in a specially designed seat on the back of the catapult arm. Then he pushes a button to set things in motion. Just like that, a huge amount of water is forced under the seat, pushing the catapult arm up and launching the rider airborne.

the science spot

So just what makes a cannonball send out such a super-sized splash? As soon as your curled-up body hits the pool, water is displaced, or pushed out of the way. The only place for that extra water to go is up and out of the pool...and all over your nearby (and formerly dry) friends!

At a Glance

Try not to grimace in pain at the thought of these splashdiving moves

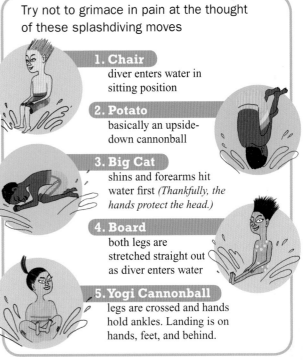

1. Chair
diver enters water in sitting position

2. Potato
basically an upside-down cannonball

3. Big Cat
shins and forearms hit water first (*Thankfully, the hands protect the head.*)

4. Board
both legs are stretched straight out as diver enters water

5. Yogi Cannonball
legs are crossed and hands hold ankles. Landing is on hands, feet, and behind.

In the Ring

NORMALLY, GRABBING HOLD OF A PERSON while they're in a pool is a bad idea. But it's the only way to go in the soggy sport of underwater wrestling, also known as aquathlon. Invented in the 1980s by a Russian swimming coach, this activity features two competitors grappling in a wrestling ring on the bottom of a pool. In the classic version of the sport, each opponent wears either a red or yellow ribbon attached to an ankle band on the leg. The wrestlers tussle, trying to tear off the opponent's ribbon. If successful, the wrestler heads to the surface and is awarded three points.

underwater wrestling: it's a duel for the drenched

Get Ready to Rumble!

For those looking for a more challenging bout, there's scuba underwater wrestling. Played in the same kind of ring as a classic match, opponents in these bouts wear a mask, weight belt, and scuba tank. The pair square off at the bottom of the pool. This time the object is to push your opponent into the area of water that surrounds the ring.

are you serious?

Every year in Rossendale, England, several hundred people come out for the World Gravy Wrestling Championships. As you might have guessed, contestants wrestle in a pool of gravy. The winner of each two-minute match is determined by who gets the most applause from the crowd. Participants wear funny costumes and try out unusual moves, all to get the audience on their side.

👉 INSIDE THE RULE BOOK:

This sport isn't like pro wrestling, where just about anything goes. In underwater wrestling, there's no punching, choking, or intentionally tearing off swimsuits, masks, or fins. Play nice!

Take this quiz

Head in to the ring and figure out which of these moves are only found in the wild world of pro wrestling.

1. **Bulldog**
2. **Moonsault**
3. **Seatbelt single**
4. **Dragonrana**
5. **Cross face cradle**
6. **Mule kick**
7. **Hip heist**

The strictly pro wrestling moves are: 1, 2, and 4.

HERE'S TO HISTORY

The first wrestling match is believed to have occurred at the ancient Olympics in 708 BC. At the time, there were two versions of the sport. In upright wrestling, the object was to throw an opponent to the ground. A wrestler was officially defeated after three falls. In ground wrestling, it didn't matter if a wrestler's whole body ended up on the ground. The only way to be victorious was for a rival to admit defeat. To do this, he pointed his index finger at the umpire. Say "uncle"!

💡 invention dimension

If the idea of taking part in a wrestling match leaves you tied up in knots, maybe thumb wrestling is more up your alley. An American artist has created a wrestling mat especially for the thumb wrestlers of the world. The Thumb War Card features two holes, one for each competitor's thumb. The clever mat makes cheating pretty well impossible. One, two, three, four...I declare a thumb war!

He Shoots
He Swims

QUICK—WHAT'S THE FIRST THING that comes to mind when you think about hockey? A hockey player, a puck, a slapshot...how about a bathing suit? Probably not. But that's on the list of things to wear in underwater hockey, or octopush as it's also known. In this noncontact sport, two teams compete against each other on the bottom of a swimming pool. To begin a match, players wait against the walls in the water. At the sound of the buzzer, they take a deep breath, dive down, and swim after the puck.

underwater hockey: swap the skates for snorkels

Into the Deep

Just like in hockey, players try to maneuver the puck into the opposing team's net. But in this game, they use a short stick to push the puck across the pool bottom toward a goalie-free net. To catch a quick breath during the action, players wear a snorkel. This allows them to watch what's going on in the game while they hover at the surface for a few moments of air time.

LEAVE IT TO THE PROS!

SPORTS TO SPARE

How do you take hockey to the extreme? Well, you can play it under water...or under ice. A small group of crazy hockey players in Austria use the underside of a frozen pond as a "rink." Players wear wetsuits and flippers and dive into an opening in the ice. Then they push a floating puck under the ice. Participants must swim to an air hole every 30 seconds to take in a fresh gulp of oxygen. And since the game is extremely dangerous, it's supervised by four scuba divers who carry oxygen with them. Sounds like an all-around bad idea.

At a Glance

Stickhandle through the differences between hockey and underwater hockey.

	ICE HOCKEY	UNDERWATER HOCKEY
Year it was first played	most likely in the late 1800s in Montreal, Canada	invented in 1954 by English diver Alan Blake
Number of players	six players on ice for each team, including a goalie	each team has six players, but no goalie
Playing time	three 20-minute periods	two halves that are between 10 to 15 minutes each
Attire	team uniforms, skates, helmet, and heavy padding (including shoulder pads, elbow pads, gloves, and shin guards)	swimsuit, swim cap, diving masks, a snorkel, and flippers
Stick	long stick with slender shaft and a flat blade on one end	short, curved stick—usually about 35 cm (1.2 ft.) long—that is sometimes called a pusher. White or black depending on team.
Puck	black disc made of hard rubber	brightly colored disc that's about the same size as ice hockey puck but is made of lead
Net	has posts, crossbar, and netting enclosure on it	commonly made from aluminum or stainless steel and looks more like a gutter
Penalties	can range from two minutes to an ejection from the game. Fouls include: hooking, high sticking, boarding, and tripping.	can range from a team moving back 3 m (10 ft.) from the puck to an ejection from the game. Fouls include: using the stick against someone and blocking an opposing player.
Referees	two referees and two linesmen are on the ice to enforce the rules and keep the game running smoothly	two or three referees in the pool who wear a distinctive cap and T-shirt. One or more poolside deck refs track time, keep score, and call fouls.

Strange Moments in Sports

Take a look at some of the wackiest moments that have taken place in the sports world.

CHEATER, CHEATER, PUMPKIN EATER

It was April 21, 1980, and a Cuban woman was the first female to cross the finish line at that year's Boston Marathon. She ran the race in just over two-and-a-half hours, faster than any woman had ever done before. Except, she had barely broken a sweat and wasn't breathing heavily after the grueling race. Marathon organizers investigated and discovered the woman had snuck into the race near the finish line!

CASE OF THE DISAPPEARING BALL

It's hard to play a football game when you can't actually see the ball. The Winnipeg Blue Bombers and Hamilton Tiger-Cats of the Canadian Football League were playing a championship match in December of 1962 when things took a turn for the weird. During the second quarter, a thick fog rolled over the field. The fog got so heavy that players couldn't see the ball, so officials had to suspend play until the next afternoon.

MASTER OF DISGUISE

Football fan Jerry Marlowe loves to catch his old college team, the Ohio State Buckeyes, take on the rival team from Michigan. But just for fun, Marlowe never pays for a ticket. Since the 1970s, he has been sneaking into the Ohio State–Michigan games dressed in costumes that have included: a team doctor, a ref, a TV cameraman, and a cheerleader. Marlowe was only caught one time. He was dressed as an usher.

I'LL GET THERE SOMEDAY

When Mexican skier Roberto Alvarez raced in the 50-km cross-country skiing event at the 1988 Winter Olympics, he was at a bit of a disadvantage. Since he lives in sunny Mexico, he didn't have a lot of skiing experience. He finished in last place, almost an hour behind the 60th place finisher. Olympic officials were so concerned about Alvarez that they sent a search party out onto the course!

BREAK A...NECK?

In 1956, a soccer goalie named Bert Trautmann showed he was all guts when he played in a championship game with a broken neck. With his team leading, Trautmann dove to make a save. He was hit by an opponent's knee and knocked out. Since substitutions weren't allowed, Trautmann carried on after he came to. He held the opponents scoreless, and his team won. Three days later, a doctor informed Trautmann he had a broken neck!

LET'S CALL IT A DAY...PLEASE

In April of 1981, the Rochester Red Wings and Pawtucket Red Sox were tied after nine innings. So the players continued playing. By 4 a.m. the game was still tied, the players were exhausted, and only 19 fans remained in the stands. The game was suspended in the 32nd inning after 8 hours and 25 minutes of play! It was resumed two months later, and the Sox won in the 33rd inning. It remains the longest game in baseball history.

IF AT FIRST YOU DON'T SUCCEED...

In 1912, an American golfer named Maud McInnes took 166 strokes on a golf hole that should have taken just three. In fact, her ball even ended up in a river. Not one to give up, McInnes hopped into a boat and had her husband paddle after the wayward ball. She managed to swipe it onto dry land and eventually completed the hole. Give her an "A" for effort!

WHAT A FAKE-OUT

As part of the tradition of modern Olympic Games, runners throughout the world take turns carrying the Olympic torch. But in 1956, an Australian student decided to pull a fast one. During the Sydney leg of the torch's journey, the mischievous man made a fake torch using a wooden chair leg topped with a burning pair of underwear. Surprisingly, police officers helped him make his way through the crowds, so he could present the torch to the mayor. Once he'd passed off the fake, the man ran off.

103

Chapter 5

Catch a Chill

There's a chill in the air. No, wait. That's not a chill, that's a warm **weird** front moving in. From *golfing on ice* to *kayaking down a mountain*, these winter sports will bring out the **yeti** in you.

The Coolest Race Around

RUNNING IN A MARATHON is challenging enough. But just imagine tossing extreme subzero temperatures into the mix. In the North Pole Marathon, which was first held in 2002, participants head to one of the remotest places on Earth and run 42 km (26.2 mi.) across the snowy and icy ground. Runners face bone-chilling temperatures of -30°C (-22°F) or less, and that's not their only challenge. The ground at the North Pole is uneven because of ice cracks and soft snow. In fact, these conditions can be so bad that athletes sometimes have to run in snowshoes!

north pole marathon: who wouldn't like to go for a run around Santa's home base?

At a Glance

- **GETTING THERE:** Runners fly to an island off the coast of Norway. From there, a second jet flies them to the North Pole Camp.

- **COST:** The entry fee for the North Pole Marathon is about $16,000 US. This includes flights, hotels, medals, and souvenirs.

- **COURSE:** The North Pole Marathon follows a circular route with flags along the way to guide athletes. Participants must run around this course 10 times.

- **TERRAIN:** This is the only marathon that is run on water—or at least the frozen water of the Arctic Ocean. The ice measures up to 3.7 m (12 ft.) thick.

- **ALONG THE ROUTE:** Large heated tents are located on the route so that runners can warm up.

- **TEMPERATURE:** It's possible for temperatures to hit -30°C (-22°F) or even lower.

- **SAFETY FIRST:** There are doctors along the race who check each competitor regularly to make sure nobody has signs of frostbite or snow blindness.

HERE'S TO HISTORY

It's generally accepted that American explorer Robert E. Peary was the first person to reach the North Pole. He arrived at the pole on April 6, 1909, after a grueling journey by dogsled, along with another explorer named Matthew Henson and four Inuit. There is, however, some controversy over whether Peary made it as far as the official North Pole. Some argue that American explorer Dr. Frederick Cook actually discovered the pole in April 1908.

 # the science spot

No matter where you stand on Earth, you can hold a compass and its needle will point to the North Pole. Just how does that happen? The Earth is like a giant magnet. It has a north and south magnetic pole. When it comes to magnets, the general rule is that opposite poles attract each other, while like poles repel. A needle of a compass is magnetically attracted to the North Pole, so it always points north.

SPORT SHORTS

Because of the nasty threat of frostbite, organizers of the North Pole Marathon advise that layering clothes is the best way to keep your hands, feet, and face protected. It's also a good idea for marathon runners to wear goggles to protect against snow blindness.

SPORTS TO SPARE

If the thought of running in the freezing cold doesn't get you lacing up your shoes, maybe racing through the desert is more your style. The Marathon Des Sables (also known as the Marathon of the Sands) is a six-day marathon that takes place each year on the Sahara Desert in Morocco. With temperatures peaking at a blistering 49°C (120°F), runners must carry all their belongings and food in a backpack for this 250 km (156 mi.) run. And the heat isn't the only challenge. In 1994, an Italian man taking part in the marathon got disoriented when a sandstorm hit. He ended up lost in the Sahara for nine days before he was rescued!

Downhill and Dangerous

SOME SAY IT'S A COMBINATION of downhill skiing, roller derby, and BMX. Let's just say it's two kinds of crazy. Downhill ice cross, which is also known as crashed ice, is an extreme sport that got its start in 2001. It features four skaters careening down a steep, icy course at speeds topping 70 kmh (44 mph). The participants, who are mainly hockey players from around the world, dress in hockey gear as they go shoulder-to-shoulder battling to be the first to the bottom of the course.

downhill ice cross: think downhill skiing on ice... with skates instead of skis

Cruising a Crazy Course

A downhill ice cross track is nothing if not challenging. It's packed with hairpin turns, bumps, jumps, and other obstacles along the way. While players try to boldly muscle their way through the course, athletes are expected to play by the rules. They're not allowed to trip or hold on to another racer's shirt. These types of infractions will get a racer disqualified from the competition.

Making the Ice

It's no easy feat putting together a course for a downhill ice cross race. For starters, a crew constructs the skeleton of the track from scratch. Once that's done, the ice makers take over. Specially designed ice mats are laid down in the track. These mats contain cooling tubes that'll keep the ice solid for racers. The crew then floods the course to form the ice. The layers of ice are carefully built up to ensure a smooth surface. Of course, getting rid of the track is easier. Special machines pump heat and the ice disappears within about eight hours!

SPORTS TO SPARE

Ski cross is the sport that's most like downhill ice cross. In this wintertime diversion, four skiers swoosh down a hill that features jumps, twists, and turns. The first skier to the bottom wins the race. As with ice cross, racers in this sport aren't allowed to push or pull. But with the high speeds and twisting courses, crashes are a common part of the action-packed competition.

the science spot

You put an ice cube tray full of water in the freezer and in a matter of hours you have ice. What's the science behind it? Water molecules are always moving and bouncing off one another. But as water cools down, its molecules start to move more slowly. Once the water temperature reaches around 0°C (32°F), the molecules stick together and form a solid, otherwise known as ice.

are you serious?

Sometimes there doesn't have to be a chill in the air to lace up your ice skates. Every November for nearly 10 years, one hotel in Southern California has set up an outdoor skating rink just steps from the beach. The ice rink overlooks the Pacific Ocean and is even surrounded by palm trees. And, best of all, there's no need to bundle up while you skate, since the temperature outside is summery.

109

Snowy Cycling

winter cycling:
gear up for a spin
in the snow

MOST PEOPLE PUT THEIR BIKES in storage
for the winter. But there are some determined
cyclists who don't let the snow slow them
down. In ice bike racing, riders take their
two-wheelers on snowmobile trails, as well as
frozen lakes and rivers. Using mountain bikes
equipped with spiked tires, these racers ride
and slide on twisting courses that have been
cut from a blanket of snow.

How to...
Bike in the Snow

Gear up to find out how biking experts handle winter on their wheels.

1. Stay seated for more control.
2. Scan ahead down the trail. You never know when a patch of ice may slip you up.
3. If your bike starts to veer sideways, don't oversteer. Make small corrections instead.
4. Sometimes well-worn tracks can be icy, so go around them and use fresh snow on the edge of the trail.
5. To prevent wipeouts, don't lean into turns. But prepare for a little skidding as you turn, just like when you're riding through gravel or sand.
6. If you hit a patch of ice, stop pedaling. You may need to use a foot to steady yourself.

Take this quiz

Cruise in and match up these types of bikes with their description:

1. RICKSHAW
2. RECUMBENT BIKE
3. FOLDING BIKE
4. TANDEM BIKE
5. MONOWHEEL

A. allows riders to sit in a reclined position

B. designed for more than one rider

C. one-wheeled ride that's similar to unicycle except cyclist sits within rim of wheel

D. three-wheeled bike that's used as a taxi in some Asian cities

E. takes up little space and can be easily carried into buildings and workspaces

Answers: 1. D; 2. A; 3. E; 4. B; 5. C

invention dimension

You're ready to roll and ski with this blizzard-friendly two-wheeler. The NIVIS snow cycle is a concept bike that's the brainchild of two German designers. It has a ski-like apparatus on the front of the bike. And, instead of a back tire, the bicycle has a special gripping belt that provides traction while riding in the snow. Plus, like any other bike, this sweet ride is powered by pedaling.

SPORTS TO SPARE

For those who don't really want to go full-out on a bike in the snow, there is an alternative. The skibob is a specially designed bike that has skis instead of wheels. Skibobbing has been a form of transportation in the Alps for some time. But it didn't really hit the sports scene until 1954 when the first international skibobbing championships were held. Skibob riders can whip down hills at speeds topping 195 kmh (121 mph). Hold on tight!

Frozen Fun

ice golf:
put your tee
time on ice

IN THIS VERSION OF GOLF, the so-called greens aren't green at all. They're white...thanks to all the ice and snow! Believe it or not, fans of ice golfing tee off on frozen ground in the dead of winter. But surprisingly, this little known sport is not new. The snow-friendly pastime dates back to at least the 17th century. At that time, the game was played in the Netherlands and was known as "kolven."

Take a Snowy Swing

Today the World Ice Golf Championships are played annually in Greenland, which is about 600 km (373 mi.) north of the Arctic Circle. Golfers face the extreme cold as they play on a course that's framed by glaciers and huge icebergs. The ground on this golf course is hard and icy with a thin layer of powdered snow. That makes it hard to spot a white golf ball, so ice golfers use fluorescent-orange golf balls instead. Fore!

 ## the science spot

You've probably noticed those small indentations, or dimples, on the surface of a golf ball. But just why are they there? The story goes that golf balls were originally smooth, but golfers began to notice that their older, scuffed-up balls flew farther than their new ones. In 1905, a golf ball manufacturer named William Taylor began adding dimples to his design to get the same far-flying effect from new balls. Soon every golfer was using a dimpled ball. So how do dimples help a golf ball soar? As a ball sails through the sky, the dimples redirect air toward the back of the golf ball. This increase in air pressure behind the ball pushes it to fly farther.

At a Glance

Head for the greens (or whites?) to discover the differences between golf and ice golf.

	GOLF	ICE GOLF
Place and year it was first played	in Scotland in the 1400s	in the Netherlands in the 1600s on a frozen canal
Course	series of holes spread out along a grassy, landscaped area	played on frozen ground, sometimes amidst glaciers and icebergs
Clothes	common golf attire includes a shirt with collar, pants, and proper golf shoes	warm layers, boots, gloves, and sunglasses
Ball	historically, wooden and feather-filled balls. Today, they're made of layers of rubber and plastic.	orange, so they can be spotted on the snow-white course

SPORTS TO SPARE

Golf isn't the only sport that's been given a winter twist. Bundle up and check out these other activities that got the cool treatment.

SNOW SOFTBALL

Just like in softball, two teams head out to a large field to swing their bats and bring in some runs. But this version of the sport is played on a field covered with snow. Bet that makes it easier to slide home!

SNOW RUGBY

Similar to rugby, except for the obvious—it's played in deep snow. Players can throw, kick, or catch the ball to move it up the field. And all passes must be sideways or backward. The sport is played in countries including Canada, England, Latvia, and the United States.

SNOW TENNIS

In this sport, players use paddles instead of rackets, and the ball can't bounce on the ground. Players have to volley it over the net to their opponent's side of the court. This version of the sport is scored just like tennis and is played over three sets.

Head for the Hills

indoor skiing: all the fun of skiing with a roof over your head

THERE'S NO NEED TO HEAD out into Mother Nature to hit the slopes. Indoor ski resorts are popping up around the world, allowing skiers and snowboarders to find fresh powder year-round. One of these indoor ski resorts is actually found smack-dab in the hot climate of the Middle East. Open for winter fun since 2005, Ski Dubai features a mountain that's about 25 stories tall. It has five slopes, a quarter-pipe for snowboarders, and a tow lift to carry skiers up the mountain. Plus, there's an area that's strictly for tobogganing, snowball fights, and snowman making.

Come Inside...
the Snow Is Fine

If downhill skiing isn't your thing, you can try heading inside for some cross-country skiing instead. Indoor ski tunnels are made especially for this winter sport. Found mainly in Finland, Sweden, and Germany, these buildings feature snow-covered trails just like those in the great outdoors...except, of course, they have a roof overhead. Skiers from all over the world head to these tunnels to train on the curving trails and small hills.

are you serious?

You know what they say about not eating yellow snow? Well, this snow might not be yellow, but you'd probably think twice before chowing down on it anyway. The owners of a ski resort in Arizona recently announced plans to make snow for their hills using recycled sewer water from a nearby city. Since snowfalls in this desert state aren't steady, the resort needs a backup plan for those less-than-snowy days. Enter the wastewater. Before you gag, it's not quite as disgusting as it sounds. The sewage water will be treated to destroy any germs. Feel better?

SPORT SHORTS

So just how exactly is snow made for an indoor snow park? First, water and air are forced through a special contraption called a snow gun. This mixture is then blasted into the chilly air of the indoor park. When it hits the air, the mixture freezes into a fine mist and snowflakes are formed. And soon the ground is covered with the white stuff. Let the skiing begin!

 ## the science spot

You may have heard the saying that no two snowflakes are exactly alike, but is that fact or fiction? A scientist named Wilson A. Bentley was one of the first people to photograph snowflakes. He spent 40 years studying thousands of the white flecks. In all that time, he never found two identical flakes. Many things affect a snowflake's size and shape, including wind and temperature. So while it's impossible to study every snowflake that falls, it's likely that Bentley's research was accurate and that all snowflakes are one of a kind.

SPORTS TO SPARE

So you feel like skiing, but there's not a snowflake in sight? No problem. You can always try your skills at grass skiing. Invented in France in 1966, this sport features short skis that have rolling treads—similar to those found on army tanks—on the bottom. Once the skis are attached to your boots, you're ready to whoosh down the nearest grassy slope.

Hang in There

hangboarding:
a sport that combines
snowboarding and
hang gliding

HANGBOARDING IS PROBABLY THE ONLY WAY to fly
without ever leaving the ground. The sport is best
described as a combination of hang gliding and
snowboarding. To tackle a face-first journey down a
mountain, a rider attaches a device called a HangBoard
to a regular snowboard. A harness hangs from a
T-shaped bar on the HangBoard and suspends the
rider in the air. Then the brave boarder grips on to the
handlebars and—presto!—it's time to carve on down
the mountainside.

At a Glance

- **HOW DO YOU GET ON A HANGBOARD?**
  Riders slip on a vest-like harness that hangs from the frame of the board. Then they clip their feet into the rudders on the back of the rig.

- **HOW DO YOU START?** You simply push off with your hands or feet.

- **HOW DO YOU STOP?** To slow down, riders push down on both rudders at the same time. Or they can stop the way snowboarders do, by sliding up on one edge against a slope.

- **HOW FAST CAN YOU GO?** It's a speed machine! Riders can reach speeds of 100 kmh (62 mph).

- **WHAT WILL HAPPEN IF YOU CRASH?**
  Hangboarding is no riskier than skiing or snowboarding. Since riders have less distance to fall, a wipeout is generally not that big a deal. Plus, a HangBoard normally doesn't slide very far because the handlebars and rudders often stick into the snow and stop it.

SPORTS TO SPARE

Here's another sport where you tend to hang around a lot. In hang gliding, athletes are strapped into a harness that hangs below a large wing. They launch themselves off mountainsides and ride the wind. Most hang gliders soar at altitudes of approximately 1,800 m (6,000 ft.).

HERE'S TO HISTORY

This outrageous sport was invented in 2002 by a Canadian man named Don Arney. Of course, the HangBoard had to be tested. So he called on snowboard champion Everest MacDonald. MacDonald made her first run on the HangBoard before it even had a braking system! And since it was important that no one steal the HangBoard's design, the testing was kept top secret. That meant MacDonald boarded in the dead of night, sometimes with a helmet light so she could see where she was going.

A ski run or path down a mountain is known as a piste.

dare to compare

In North America, downhill ski trails are classified by a color-shape rating system:

 GREEN CIRCLE: the easiest ski runs, sometimes known as "bunny hills." Fairly flat and smooth trails.

 BLUE SQUARE: medium difficulty. Steeper and narrower than green runs.

 BLACK DIAMOND: an advanced run that often has challenging terrain. Perfect for experienced skiers.

 DOUBLE BLACK DIAMOND: for experts only. Very steep and often left in a completely natural state.

In Europe, trails are classified by color alone. These colors, which correspond to the North American system, are green, blue, red, and black.

Have a Ball

THE GROUND IS COVERED in a blanket of freshly fallen snow. You're walking along with your friend when—whack!— a snowball hits you in the back. And so it begins...snowball fight! While most snowball fights are spur-of-the-moment, some are more serious fun. In fact, snowball fighting became an organized sport called Yukigassen in Japan in 1989. In this snow free-for-all, teams of seven players battle on a field that has several shelters made of snow. While it got its start in Japan, Yukigassen tournaments are now held in Finland, Norway, Australia, Sweden, Canada, and the United States.

yukigassen: *(say: you-key-goss-en)* whose name comes from the Japanese word for "snow battle."

118

Let 'Em Have It!

The object of Yukigassen is to hit the opposing team with your snowballs. Anyone who gets pelted is eliminated from that period, and the team with the most players left at the end of the period wins that round. The first team to win two periods claims victory. That said, a team can win the battle if it captures the opposition's flag, which is found sticking out from the ground on the opposing team's side of the field.

☞ INSIDE THE RULE BOOK:

- Each team has four forward players, as well as three back players who guard the flag and pass snowballs to their teammates up ahead.
- The teams face-off in three 3-minute periods, each armed with 90 pre-made snowballs per period.
- Since a snowball to the face can make you cry like a baby, players must wear helmets with face shields.
- A player who makes a snowball from the snow on the ground is automatically eliminated.
- A referee keeps a close eye on all the snowball-throwing action.

RECORD BREAKER!

Imagine snowballs flying from every direction for as far as the eye can see. In October of 2009, a snowball fight reached epic proportions when 5,768 people gathered in a small Belgium town to pummel each other with the snowy spheres. To make sure there was enough of the cold stuff for the battle, about 120 tonnes of snow was specially shipped in to the town.

the equipment

A special snowball maker produces the 540 balls needed for a Yukigassen game. The contraption features a mold that makes 45 snowballs at once. You just put the snow in the maker, close the lid, press down hard, and voilà—you've got perfectly round snowballs ready to go...or throw!

home   shelter   team flags   •• player

The Thrill of the Hill

TIRED OF TOBOGGANING? One of the latest ways to barrel down a snowy hill is in a kayak. Yes, it's true. Snow kayakers actually drag a one-person boat to a hilltop and use it as a super-long sled. A paddle also comes along for the ride. At first it's used to push off the top of the slope. Then it comes in handy for steering the watercraft on the way down. And stopping is achieved by digging the paddle into the snow.

snow kayaking: anyone can ride a toboggan down a hill

Snow, Snow, Snow Your Boat

The Snow Kayak World Championships are held in Austria each year. About 200 kayakers from 12 countries take to the hills in their boats. And it must be pretty clear sailing the whole way down, as they can clock speeds of up to 70 kmh (44 mph).

dare to compare

Set sail and discover the differences between a canoe and a kayak.

Canoe:

- a wooden boat that's pointed at both ends and completely open on top

- paddler sits on seat or kneels on bottom of boat

- can be paddled solo or with several people onboard

- single-bladed paddle is used

- oldest known canoe was discovered in the Netherlands. It was constructed sometime between 8200 BC and 7600 BC.

Kayak:

- long boat made from plastic and usually closed on top with a cockpit for kayaker; can have two cockpits for two boaters

- paddler sits on bottom of boat

- double-bladed paddle is used

- sits very close to surface of water

- tends to be faster than a canoe and can be used in rougher waters

- kayak was first made by the Inuit as a way to hunt on the ocean. It was originally made from animal skin.

RECORD BREAKER!

You've heard of being up a creek without a paddle? Well, it's probably not half as bad as being over a waterfall with one! An American professional white-water rafter named Tyler Bradt holds the unofficial world record for kayaking over the highest waterfall successfully. In April 2009, Bradt paddled over the Palouse Falls in Washington State. The dynamic drop measured 58 m (189 ft.) and lasted four seconds. Going doowwn!

are you serious?

In 2006, an Israeli designer named Yael Mer created a skirt that turns into a kayak. Mer dreamed up the Evacuation Skirt, which is basically a portable life raft, during hurricane season. The skirt looks fashionable when it's deflated. But once inflated, it transforms into a kayak that can carry an adult woman to safety. Sail away!

invention dimension

You can toss the paddle away with this kayak. The PowerKayak has an engine that lets a boater make waves on lakes and rivers while traveling up to 40 kmh (25 mph). Of course, dedicated kayakers can paddle if they want. But we're guessing the need for speed will win out each time!

Put It on the Ice

ice yachting:
a sport for boaters
who won't let a little
ice stand in their way

IT'S SMOOTH SAILING IN THIS fast-paced wintertime activity. In ice yachting, sailboats catch the wind and glide across "hard water"—also known as ice. The bottom of an ice yacht is fitted with runners, or skates, that allow the vessel to smoothly coast over an icy surface. And a canvas sail sets the boat in motion with the help of the wind. Sailors best hold on tight during their cool ride as the boats can hit speeds of 90 kmh (56 mph).

At a Glance

- **STARTING:** A sailor stands beside the boat and positions it so that the sail catches the wind. As the boat begins to slide, the sailor jumps in and adjusts its direction, so the sail can continue to move the boat forward.

- **MANEUVERING:** To steer, sailors use a lever, called a tiller, that's found inside the boat. The tiller controls the runners on the bottom of the vessel. Steering must be done carefully, so the boat doesn't slip-slide out of control.

- **STOPPING:** To stop an ice boat, a sailor steers into the wind and lets the sail down.

HERE'S TO HISTORY

While it's considered a sport today, ice yachting wasn't always fun and games. In the 17th century, it was a mode of transportation in the Netherlands during the cold winters. At that time, sailors fastened blades to the bottom of their boats so they could move cargo across frozen lakes and rivers.

great moments in...
ice yachting

1871 The longest ice yacht ever was built in New York State. Called the Icicle, this boat measured 21 m (68.9 ft.) long. The ice craft often raced trains that ran on a track along the Hudson River in eastern New York. In fact, in 1871, the Icicle sailed to victory against a train on a 60 km (37 mi.) run.

The top speed ever recorded for an ice yacht was 135 kmh (84 mph) on a lake in Pennsylvania. An American team is currently designing a sleek, futuristic ice boat in the hopes that it can break the current high-speed record.

SPORT SHORTS

- It's important that ice sailors put safety first when they head out onto a frozen lake or river. A life jacket, helmet, and protective padding are crucial for this slip-sliding sport.

- Ice sailors always keep their eyes open for dangerous ice conditions, including open water, thin ice, and cracks. These can spell big trouble if they aren't seen in time.

SPORTS TO SPARE

Sailing isn't the only water sport that you can put on ice. Canadian windsurfers recently invented a winterized version of the sport. Called ice surfing, it features boards with skate-style blades strapped to the bottom. Like windsurfing, this sport uses a sail to catch the wind and pull you along. Unlike windsurfing, the water beneath you is frozen! To steer, surfers simply lean forward or backward on the board. While the unusual sport got its start in Canada, it has now found a following in many European countries. Ice is nice!

The Sky Life

speed flying: you can climb over a mountain or throw yourself off the side of one

HERE'S A SPORT THAT TAKES SKIING to a whole new level...namely, the sky! It's called speed flying, and it combines paragliding and skiing skills. Typically, paragliders use a special parachute, or wing, to soar off mountaintops. But speed flyers add another element to the sport—skis on their feet. With a wing and skis in tow, they climb up a mountain or have a helicopter drop them off, and then they leap off the mountainside. They land skis-first in the snow and swoosh along. Then, when a rock or ledge comes by, they use their wing to soar up, up, and away.

great moments in...
speed flying

In March of 2008, François Bon, one of the paragliders who invented speed flying, headed to Argentina to fly down the country's Aconcagua Mountains. It took him 11 days to hike up the mountainside and just 4 minutes and 50 seconds to speed fly down it!

the science spot

Avalanches are a real danger to athletes who take part in winter sports on mountains. An avalanche can be caused by many factors, including a snowstorm, high winds, or temperature changes. Once a top layer of snow breaks away and starts tumbling down the mountainside, it's pretty much impossible to escape. Consider this: an avalanche can top speeds of 130 kmh (80 mph) within just five seconds. Now that's power.

HERE'S TO HISTORY

Speed flying got its start in 2003 when five daredevils came up with the idea of soaring and skiing at the same time. By 2007, this risky pastime had turned into an organized sport with a competition in France that brought together nearly 30 flyers. Funnily enough, there were no judges. At the end of the competition, flyers gathered to watch videos of each other, and they awarded points for style and technique. Today hundreds of adrenaline-filled athletes take part in speed flying, and there are designated speed-flying slopes in the Alps. Ready for takeoff?

the equipment

According to speed-flying experts, there is some must-have equipment for the sport:

- speed flying wing
- skis
- helmet
- goggles
- avalanche transceiver emits a signal so you can be found quickly in case of an avalanche
- signal mirror to be used as a signaling device if you get into trouble and need to be rescued
- whistle also can be used to call attention to yourself if you need help

Weird World Records

Crack open the record books for a look at some of the oddest sports records around.

GIVE IT A SPIN

An American man named Michael Kettman broke the record for the most basketballs spun simultaneously in May 1999. Kettman constructed a special rack that he could lay over his legs. Then he spun 28 basketballs all at once.

DRESSED FOR SUCCESS

Orange you glad you nabbed the record? In 2009, a British woman named Sally Orange captured the record for the fastest marathon in a fruit costume. She finished the London Marathon in 4 hours, 32 minutes, 28 seconds—all while dressed as an orange. Not to be outdone, a man named Robert Prothero ran the marathon dressed as a carrot and took home the record for fastest marathon in a vegetable costume.

WHERE'S THE WATER

In September of 2008, a German woman named Maren Zönker ran away with the record for the fastest 100-m hurdles while wearing flippers. (Yes, flippers.) Zönker completed the hurdles in 22.35 seconds. No word on if she celebrated with a swim.

"CANOE" BELIEVE IT?

A group of rowers in India sailed away with the record for the largest crew on a canoe in May of 2008. The "Snake Boat" rowed along with a crew of 143—including 118 rowers, 2 rhythm men, 5 helmsmen, and 18, um, singers.

CATCH A WAVE

In October of 2009, more than one hundred surfers rode a wave on a beach in Cape Town, South Africa. They broke the record for the most surfers riding the same wave. Hang ten, everybody!

BIGSHOT BROTHERS

In August of 2008, twin brothers Ettore and Angelo Rossetti swung their way into the record books by taking part in the longest tennis rally. The sibs hit a tennis ball back and forth a total of 25,944 times. All in all, their rallying lasted 14 hours and 31 minutes.

NOW THAT'S GOTTA HURT

Baseball player Hughie Jennings was hit 51 times during the 1896 season, winning him the painful record for the most times hit by a pitch in a season. Jennings also holds the record for most times hit by a pitch in a career...at 287 times. You've got to wonder if he was standing on home plate instead of beside it!

COULDN'T YOU GO A LITTLE EASIER ON US?

She shoots, she scores...and scores...and scores...and, well, you get the picture. The record for the highest score in a hockey game happened at an Olympic qualifying match in 2008. The Slovakian women's team beat the Bulgarian squad 82–0.

LET'S HEAR YOU!

The spectators at a soccer match in Istanbul, Turkey, really blew the roof off this record in March of 2011. To break the record for the loudest crowd roar, the 51,988 fans screamed at an ear-splitting 131.76 decibels. That's almost as loud as a jet engine.

SO LONG

In September of 2008, a group of skiers nabbed the record for the longest skis around. The skis measured 534 m (1,751 ft.) long and were laid out on the main street of Örebro, Sweden. A total of 1,043 people were able to wear the skis.

Index

Photo credits

Care has been taken to trace ownership of copyright material contained in this book. Information enabling the publisher to rectify any reference or credit line in future editions will be welcomed.